Christian Meditation

Christian Meditation
Contemplative Prayer for a New Generation

PAUL HARRIS

NOVALIS

Published in North America by
Novalis
Saint Paul University
Ottawa, ON K1S 1C4 Canada

Business office:
Novalis
49 Front St. E., 2nd Floor
Toronto, ON M5E 1B3 Canada

© 1996 Paul Harris

ISBN   2 89088 866 5

Canadian Cataloguing in Publication data is available
from the National Library of Canada

Acknowledgments

Biblical quotations are taken mainly from: New English Bible, © 1961 and 1970,
Oxford University Press and Cambridge University Press; Revised Standard Version of
the Bible, © 1952 and 1971, Division of Christian Education of the National Council of
the Churches of Christ in the USA; and Jerusalem Bible, © 1967, 1968 and 1969,
Darton, Longman and Todd Ltd. and Doubleday and Co. Inc.

Printed in Canada

Contents

Preface	ix

1 Meditation as Christian prayer — 1
   A deeper way of prayer than words — 2
   Being restored to ourselves — 3
   A trinitarian prayer — 4
   Let go and let God — 5

2 Why should one meditate? — 8

3 The 'how to' of meditation — 11

4 The hunger for silence in prayer — 15

5 John Main, his life and teaching — 18
   The influence of Skellig Michael — 21

6 Scripture and meditation — 23

7 The role of Mary on the contemplative journey — 26

8 The historical roots of silence in prayer — 28
   John Cassian, the desert fathers and the hesychast tradition of prayer — 28
   The English connection: *The Cloud of Unknowing* — 31
   A continuous tradition — 34

9 The universal call to contemplative prayer — 35
   A call to all or just a chosen few? — 36
   The second hit on the head — 37
   The first shall be last and the last shall be first — 38

10 The mantra/prayer word and its role in Christian Meditation — 40
   Choosing the mantra — 43
   Other Christian mantras — 44
   Changing one's mantra — 45
   The continuous recitation of the mantra — 45

Saying the mantra at other times 46
The poverty of the mantra 47

11 The mantra, distractions and the monkey mind 49

The role of the mantra in dealing with distractions 49
Why saying the mantra is often so difficult:
the light at the end of the tunnel 52

12 The body in meditation 55

The relationship between yoga and meditation 56
Posture in prayer 57
Breathing and meditation 58
The physiological benefits of meditation 60

13 The practice of Christian Meditation 61

The time and place for meditation 61
Children and meditation 62
Meditation and self hypnosis 63
Music and meditation 64
The importance of the 'heart' in meditation 65
Taking off one's shoes while meditating 66
Meditating more than twice a day 66
Falling asleep during meditation 67
Psychic phenomena, visions and voices 68
On missing one's daily meditation period 69
Interior silence is not a void 69
God's language is silence 70
Sacred places to meditate 70
On insights during meditation 70
The gift of tears 71
Neither male nor female 71
Measuring the spiritual 73

14 Christian Meditation and other ways of prayer 75

Praying and praying for . . . 75
Different schools of contemplative prayer 76
Meditation and other ways of prayer 77
Meditation and its relationship to the
charismatic movement 78
Christian and Transcendental Meditation 79

15 Christian Meditation and unity with other faiths 82

We meet in the cave of the heart 83
Beyond East and West 84

CONTENTS

Bede Griffiths and the spiritual bridge
between the world's religions — 85

16 Meditation and action – both sides of the same coin — 87
- The inner eye of love — 87
- Love of silence and compassion for others — 90
- The fruits of prayer — 91
- Escaping or encountering reality — 92

17 From brokenness to wholeness – on the path of meditation — 95
- A time for inner healing — 95
- The woman at the well — 98

18 Commitment and perseverance on the path of meditation — 101
- The desert experience — 101
- To climb the mountain of the Lord — 106

19 The role of the Christian Meditation group — 112
- The weekly group meeting — 112
- Starting a group — 114
- Small is beautiful — 115

20 Some other aspects of the journey — 117
- Our image of God — 117
- Sharing the teaching — 119
- The prayerful reading of Scripture — 120
- The role of a teacher — 121
- Spiritual guidance and the soul friend — 121
- Smashing the mirror of the ego: leaving self behind — 124
- Keep death before one's eyes — 127
- The need to forgive — 129
- Humility and gratitude — 129
- The human consciousness of Christ — 130

21 The role of the World Community for Christian Meditation — 132
- Epilogue — 134
- Bibliography and sources cited — 135
- Name index — 139
- Subject index — 142
- The World Community for Christian Meditation — 145

Preface

Since his death on 30 December 1982, Benedictine monk John Main's teaching on silence and stillness in prayer has spread around the globe to embrace a world-wide community of meditators. This rebirth of the practice of contemplative prayer is attracting people from varying religious traditions, men and women, young and old, rich and poor, to the practice of this faith-filled daily spiritual discipline that was practised by desert monks in the earliest centuries of Christianity.

Over 1,000 Christian Meditation groups that meet weekly are now flourishing in 50 countries of the world. Because of this growth many people feel John Main's teaching is playing a vital role in the contemporary contemplative renewal of Christianity which is still only in its early days. The Christian's understanding of the importance of *stillness* in prayer is just being reawakened. John Main once said 'we have had a biblical renewal, a liturgical renewal, what we need now is a renewal in prayer'. He was also fully aware that without this spiritual discipline and experience of prayer, religion simply shrivels away in sterile moralism, ritualism, meaningless theological debate or empty observance of rules.

We are now experiencing that inner renewal. It has been said that in every age God raises up prophets and teachers to ensure his work is carried on. This book is a response to the influence of John Main's teaching on prayer that makes this Benedictine monk one of the major spiritual teachers of the twentieth century. And for this reason I have started off each chapter with a succinct quotation from this remarkable guide and communicator of this tradition of prayer.

It was John Main's custom at the conclusion of his talks on Christian Meditation to encourage his listeners to ask questions pertaining to the teaching. While never failing to urge his listeners 'to enter into the experience of meditation itself', he nevertheless was aware that for head-centred Westerners, a conceptual understanding of meditation was a prerequisite for their 'leap of faith' into the practice. Moreover, answering questions has been a long teaching tradition in Christianity. In Chapter 7 of the first letter to the Corinthians, St Paul answers specific questions from the Greek community sent on to him orally or in writing.

It is in this tradition that *Christian Meditation: Contemplative Prayer For a New Generation* is offered not only to those wishing to know more about this prayer tradition but also to those who are already meditating. As John Main once said, in meditation we are all beginners and we begin again each day. I hope this book reflects a part of John Main's deep and yet simple teaching on Christian Meditation for newcomers as well as responding to obstacles and blocks experienced by those already on the path.

Many of the points and concerns addressed in this book were raised as questions in recent years as I have given retreats, seminars and conferences on Christian Meditation in various countries of the world.

Of course the fruitfulness of this book will depend on the *experiential* aspect of meditation, and on those readers who will seek inner stillness through the daily spiritual discipline of meditation. As John Main never tired of saying, it is never sufficient simply to talk or read about meditation. In fact meditation is really not taught, nor can it really be logically explained. Nor can it be analysed or dissected. There is a saying that it is not *taught* but *caught*.

Contemplation, another term for meditation, as John Main teaches it, does not lend itself to dogmatic definition like other kinds of theology. So please note this is not an official catechism on the practice of Christian Meditation! This book simply reflects my own response to the basic issues and questions people raise; and questions that have arisen in my own practice of meditation. Other meditators answering these issues might respond in quite different ways. Every person's journey is unique, but we can share the uniqueness of the journey with each other.

Perhaps the most profound statement John Main ever made was that he could sum up the practice of Christian Meditation in three simple words 'say your mantra'. I hope this truth becomes apparent in this book as readers enter more deeply into the *experience* of silence and stillness itself and are led to that 'country beyond words and beyond names'.

PAUL HARRIS

1
Meditation as Christian prayer

Meditation is a way of coming to your own centre, coming to the foundation of your own being, and remaining there – still, silent, attentive. Meditation is in essence a way of learning to become awake, to be fully alive and be still. The way to that wakefulness is silence and stillness. This is quite a challenge for people of our time, because most of us have very little experience of silence, and silence can be terribly threatening to people in the transistorised culture that we live in. You have to get used to that silence. That is why the way of meditation is a way of learning to say a word interiorly in your heart.

I think what all of us have to learn is not so much that we have to create silence. The silence is there within us. What we have to do is to enter into it, to become silent, to become the silence. The purpose of meditation and the challenge of meditation is to allow ourselves to become silent enough to allow this interior silence to emerge. Silence is the language of the spirit.

Learning to say your mantra, learning to say your word, leaving behind all other words, ideas, imagination and fantasies, is learning to enter into the presence of the spirit who dwells in your inner heart, who dwells there in love. The Spirit of God dwells in our hearts in silence. And, in humility and in faith, we must enter into that silent presence.

*The all-important aim in Christian meditation is to allow God's mysterious and silent presence within us to become more and more not only **a** reality, but **the** reality in our lives; to let it become that reality which gives meaning, shape and purpose to everything we do, to everything we are.*

(JOHN MAIN, *Word Into Silence*)

The way of Christian Meditation is illuminated by two quotations. The first quotation is the words of Jesus from Luke 17.20–21: 'The Kingdom of God does not come in such a way as to be seen. No one will say "look here it is", or "there it is" because the Kingdom of God is within you.' And then there are these unforgettable words of St Augustine (350–430):

> O Beauty ever ancient, ever new.
> Too late have I loved you.
> I was outside and you were within me.
> And I never found you.
> Until I found you within myself.

These two quotations are about an inner journey, about the path of Christian Meditation in which we seek God in the silence and stillness of our own heart in daily periods of prayer. And as John Main tells us, it is in the silence and stillness of meditation that God in some mysterious way reveals his love for us.

In ages past coming to an inner silence and stillness in prayer was referred to as contemplative prayer. Today it is pursued by many who practice what we call meditation in the Christian tradition. If one were to define the practice of Christian Meditation one could say it is a daily spiritual discipline which leads one to attention, to concentration, to silence, to God. So meditation is much more than another method of prayer, it is about pure faith. It is really a surrender of one's whole being to God. However it is more a question of what God does than what we do. Meditation in reality is entering into the prayer of Jesus to the Father in the Spirit deep within us. And as John Main says we are swept along in this prayer of the Trinity. While in effect we are doing very little in meditation from our own willpower or resources, a deeper force within us is doing everything. The Spirit prays within us.

The experience of so many who have begun to meditate is that through meditation we can find God at the centre of our own hearts and that our lives are transformed by that discovery, by that experience. The great sixteenth-century Carmelite St John of the Cross (1542–91) says, 'God is the centre of my soul'. Julian of Norwich (1342–1416) says 'God is the still point at my centre'. Meditation is this daily pilgrimage to one's own centre and a way of living from this deep centre of one's being.

A deeper way of prayer than words

A question often asked by newcomers is whether meditation is really prayer. We are so used to a different understanding of prayer, of 'getting our prayers in'. But there is a deeper way of prayer than mere words. Jesus indicates this when he says: 'In your prayers do not babble on as the pagans do who feel that by their many words they will be heard. Do not be like them. Your Heavenly Father already knows what you need before you ask him' (Matt. 6:7–8).

St Paul gives us a further hint of what prayer is all about when he says: 'We do not know how to pray, but the Spirit prays within us' (Rom. 8:26). The more we study Scripture, the more we realise that being silent and still in prayer is at the heart of the Gospel message and of the Christian life. (See Chapter 6 on the scriptural basis of Christian Meditation.)

A fourth-century desert monk Evagrius once wrote this famous definition of prayer: 'Prayer is raising the mind and heart to God through the laying aside of thoughts.' That is what we do in meditation. We go beyond words and thoughts to rest in the Lord and to allow God to pray within us.

Psalm 116:9 says: 'I will walk in the presence of the Lord in the land of the living.' By becoming silent in this 'wordless and imageless prayer' we deepen our awareness of God's presence in our lives and we acknowledge our complete dependence on him. It was in the silence of the desert that God spoke to Moses and it is in the depths of our own silence that God speaks his prayer within us. As John Main said, it is not so much 'my prayer' that matters as the prayer of Jesus into which we are led.

Being restored to ourselves

St Augustine put the spiritual life in a beautiful way when he said: 'We must first be restored to ourselves, that, making of oneself as it were a stepping-stone, we may rise thence and be borne up to God.'

John Main reminds us that meditation is not primarily a way of *doing* but is a way of *becoming*, becoming ourselves and coming to self-knowledge. He says that in this way of prayer we seek to become the person we are called to be, that meditation is not about *doing* but about *being*. St Clement of Alexandria (150–211) echoed this when he said 'He who knows his self knows God'.

Meister Eckhart (1260–1327), the great medieval spiritual teacher, also recognised that the question of God is also a question about self-knowledge. He says that we cannot know God unless we first know ourselves and we can only know ourselves by a return to the human heart. In the book *Meister Eckhart, The Way of Paradox*, he is quoted as saying: 'The sublime and glorious reality which we call God, is to be sought first and foremost in the human heart. If we do not find him there, we shall not find him anywhere else. If we do find him there, we can never lose him again; wherever we turn, we shall see his face.' That is what we do in meditation; we seek God in our own heart and everywhere we turn (in our daily life) we see his face.

A trinitarian prayer

John Main elaborates on meditation as trinitarian prayer in one of his talks when he says:

> The Prayer of Jesus is just like a rushing torrent flowing between Jesus and the Father. What we have to do is to plunge ourselves into that and be swept along by it. It is a torrent of love, not a torrent of words and that is why we have to learn to be totally silent.
>
> (JOHN MAIN, *Being On The Way*)

Christian prayer is about entering into this prayer of Christ, into the life, the risen life of the glorified humanity of Christ and following his way to the Father. John's gospel is all about an inner Christ: 'The Father dwells in me . . . The Father and I are one . . . He who has seen me has seen the father . . . Do you not believe that I am in the Father and the Father is in me?' (John 14:10, 10:30, 14:9–10) 'If anyone loves me we will come to him and make our home in him' (John 14:23). Meditation is participating in this love that flows between the persons of the Trinity.

Thomas Merton (1915–1968) in his booklet *What is Contemplation?* points out that the promise of Jesus that he and the Father would come to abide with us 'is essentially the same beatitude as the blessed enjoy in heaven'.

We need to understand that this prayer of the Trinity is already present within us; the reality of the Kingdom is already present in the centre of our being. We simply need to become conscious of this reality. The fourteenth-century Julian of Norwich, one of the greatest trinitarians, helps us here. She says: 'where Jesus appears the blessed Trinity is understood.'

St Irenaeus put this trinitarian prayer in another way. He says that the Spirit comes to seize us and give us to the Son and the Son gives us to the Father. Whatever way we understand it meditation ultimately reveals itself as the silent life of the Trinity praying within us.

Isaac the Syrian, a sixth-century monk and bishop, once wrote:

> When the Spirit has come to reside in someone, that person cannot stop praying; for the Spirit prays without ceasing in him. No matter if he is asleep or awake, prayer is going on in his heart all the time. He may be eating or drinking, he may be resting or working – the incense of prayer will ascend spon-

taneously from his heart . . . The slightest stirring of his heart is like a voice which sings in silence and in secret to the Invisible.

Let go and let God

'Letting go' is a description of a process we go through on the path of meditation. Not only do we try to let go of words, thoughts and images but also we try to let go of our concerns, fears and anxieties during our times of meditation. We even let go of trying to make the silence happen. It is also about letting go of 'getting anywhere'. (See Chapter 13 on *not* evaluating our progress in meditation.)

We must also let go of instant results. It has been said we live in an 'instant results' society; everything from instant coffee, sameday service, to wanting to know immediately whether we have won the lottery. Our society is accomplishment and win orientated. We have a fixation on achieving goals, seeing results immediately and winning.

The Chinese spiritual philosopher Chuang Tzu (369–286 BC) saw the danger of 'results' in his poem called 'The Need to Win' translated by Thomas Merton.

> When an archer is shooting for nothing
> He has all his skill.
> If he shoots for a brass buckle
> He is already nervous.
> If he shoots for a prize of gold
> He goes blind
> Or sees two targets –
> He is out of his mind!
>
> His skill has not changed. But the prize
> Divides him. He cares.
> He thinks more of winning
> Than of shooting –
> And the need to win
> Drains him of power.

This is why John Main keeps insisting on 'letting go' of expectations, of goals, of results and in fact 'of winning' on the path of meditation.

A priest looking for results once went to John Main and said 'I've been meditating now for seven years, how long is it going to take me to come to any kind of silence?' Father John, with a twinkle in his eye, said '20 years'. And the priest in telling this story said 'and just think I have only 13 more years to go'. The point of the story being that we must have the faith of a child and give up our adult self-concern about goals and about getting somewhere. Meditation is really just the opposite. It is about letting go of our self-concerns, and it's about letting go of 'getting anywhere'.

Letting go is also freeing ourselves from our inordinate attachments. We either let go of our attachments in the silence of meditation or in death. But the great joy of the meditator is that this process can begin before death when we begin to 'let go' in our daily life and in our times of meditation; letting go of all the things we cling to, all our attachments. We must let go of all our security, our attachment to health, material possessions, reputation, everything. We are going on a journey and we must travel light. This is what Jesus meant when he said to his disciples, 'take no gold, nor silver, nor copper in your belts, no bag for your journey, nor two tunics, nor sandals, nor a staff' (Matt. 10:9–10).

St John of the Cross had this to say about detachment and 'letting go'.

> In order to have pleasure in everything
> Desire to have pleasure in nothing.
>
> In order to arrive at possessing everything
> Desire to possess nothing.
>
> In order to arrive at being everything
> Desire to be nothing.
>
> In order to arrive at knowing everything
> Desire to know nothing.
> (The Collected Works of John of the Cross)

The point John of the Cross makes is that in God we possess all things, but in order to possess God we must give up possession of everything that is less than God. We must give up all our *desires* and, having done that, everything is given to us. 'Letting go' frees us from all desires that are not centred in God. It is what John Cassian meant by non-possessiveness or 'poverty of Spirit' (see Chapter 8 on John Cassian).

Again this 'letting go' is aptly expressed by St John of the Cross in his poem 'The Dark Night':

> I abandoned and forgot myself,
> Laying My Face on my Beloved;

All things ceased; I went out from myself,
Leaving my cares
Forgotten among the lilies.

(The Collected Works of John of the Cross)

2
Why should one meditate?

It is very difficult to try to determine what it is that makes a person want to meditate. It has puzzled me over the years. There seem to be so many reasons why people start to meditate. But I think there is only one reason that keeps people meditating. That I think we could describe as a growing commitment to reality.

In God we are and we know ourselves to be lovable and loved. This is the supreme reality that Jesus came to reveal, to communicate, to live and to establish. It is established in our hearts, if only we will be open to it. This openness is what our meditation is all about. It is only from this love and with this love that we can rightly understand ourselves and all creation. Without rootedness in love, all we can see will be shadows and phantoms and we will never be able to make contact with them because they have no reality.

Meditation is the invitation to journey deeply into your own heart, into your own being. What the traditional wisdom tells us is that only with such depth of experience and vision can we live our lives in real harmony with what is.

The purpose of our meditation is that there should be nothing false in us, only reality. Only love. Only God.

(JOHN MAIN, *The Way of Unknowing*)

Meditation is built upon a simple principle, namely that our *finite* minds cannot grasp the *infinity* of God. Theology, philosophy or any other form of knowledge only tells us things *about* God. They do not bring us into the experience of God himself. God simply cannot be grasped or known by the senses. The senses are involved with the world of space and time, but God is beyond space and time. However, when words, images and ideas are abandoned, in silence we can come to an intuitive knowledge and love of God.

The practice of Christian Meditation has its origin and its meaning in the human heart. If we do not find God there we will not find him elsewhere.

WHY SHOULD ONE MEDITATE?

So how do we find God in the human heart? One answer is through this spiritual discipline of daily meditation. The late Benedictine monk Bede Griffiths (1907–93) once said that 'meditation is seeking God in the stillness beyond words or thought'. John Main has said that meditation is a way to enter the living stream of love within our own hearts and that the silence each of us is summoned to enter is the eternal silence of God. This silence, says John Main, each one of us can find within ourselves.

The essence of meditation then is our innate longing and need for God, we are waiting on God, we are listening to God, we are open to God. We throw ourselves into the arms of God. And then indeed we find the Kingdom of God is within us. And as St Augustine said, 'you have made us for yourself O Lord, and our hearts are restless until they rest in thee'.

Meditation is nothing less than the transformation of our heart as echoed in this wisdom of the desert father who said:

> Unless there is a still center in the middle of the storm. Unless a person in the midst of all their activities preserves a secret room in their heart where they stand alone before God, unless we do this we will lose all sense of spiritual direction and be torn to pieces.
>
> (KALLISTOS WARE, *Theology and Prayer*)

When we meditate we go into that secret place, that still centre. And out of that stillness where we are turned towards God, comes the life of the Spirit where we are transformed into love. We Christians meditate to open ourselves to the birth of Christ within.

Henry Wadsworth Longfellow (1807–82) echoed this opening to God in silence:

> Let us, then, labor for an inward stillness –
> An inward stillness and an inward healing;
> That perfect silence where the lips and heart
> Are still, and we no longer entertain
> Our own imperfect thoughts and vain opinions,
> But God alone speaks in us, and we wait
> In singleness of heart, that we may know
> His will, and in silence of our spirits,
> That we may do his will, and do that only.

Why do we meditate? Because in meditation God is working deep in our soul. On this spiritual path he is cleansing our soul from our failings and imperfections, sanctifying us and increasing his divine life within us. He is doing it within us because we have left ourselves completely at his disposal, not getting in his way. We leave him completely free to do his work. We are like musical instruments and God is the musician. We are at God's disposal and God plays upon us whatever melody he wishes. This is not, however, mere passivity. To be open to the divine music demands total self-acceptance.

Why do we meditate? Because in meditation the fruits of prayer enter our life almost immediately and if we persevere on the path of meditation, the love of God overflows in our life like a reservoir. These fruits of prayer, the fruits of the spirit as St Paul terms them include 'love, joy, peace, patience, kindness, generosity, faithfulness, gentleness, self-control' (Gal. 5:22–24). This love will overflow in our lives in a thousand ways. But John Main reminds us that we can become intoxicated by words. The only important thing is to enter daily into the experience itself in faithfulness and commitment. The experience itself will teach us more about the 'why' of meditation.

3
The 'how to' of meditation

Sit down. Sit still and upright. Close your eyes lightly. Sit relaxed but alert. Silently, interiorly begin to say a single word. We recommend the prayer-phrase 'maranatha'. Recite it as four syllables of equal length. Listen to it as you say it, gently but continuously. Do not think or imagine anything – spiritual or otherwise. If thoughts and images come, these are distractions at the time of meditation, so keep returning to simply saying the word. Meditate each morning and evening for between twenty and thirty minutes.

(JOHN MAIN, *The Way of Unknowing*)

The thing that surprises most newcomers to Christian Meditation is its *simplicity*. John Main always emphasised how simple it is to enter into the *experience* of meditation.

As we begin to meditate it is good to become aware of our breathing. Let your breathing slow down and become regular and as John Main says, interiorly begin to say a single word. He recommends the ancient Christian prayer: 'Maranatha'. Recite it as he suggests in four equally stressed syllables: ma-ra-na-tha. Listen to it as you say it, gently but continuously. Maranatha means 'Come Lord Jesus'. Maranatha is an Aramaic word, the language that Jesus spoke. St Paul ends the first letter to the Corinthians with this prayer word and St John ends the book of Revelation with this word. It is one of the oldest Christian prayers. Biblical commentators tell us it was a password which allowed the early Christians into homes for the celebration of the Eucharist.

In meditation we do not think or imagine anything spiritual or otherwise. If thoughts and images come, even holy thoughts, these are distractions at the time of meditation, so we return to simply saying our word. 'Meditation', as one T-shirt put it, is 'not what you think'. *The Cloud of Unknowing* says, 'He may well be loved, but he may not be thought. He may be reached and held close by means of love, but never by means of thought.'

John Main recommends meditating each morning and evening

for between 20 and 30 minutes (20 minutes for beginners), preferably before and after the day's work. It is better to meditate before a meal.

In meditation we do not reflect on the meaning of our word as we recite it. The author of the fourteenth-century *Cloud of Unknowing* is emphatic on this point:

> If your mind begins to intellectualize over the meaning and connotations of this little word, remind yourself that its value lies in its simplicity. Do this and I assure you these thoughts will vanish . . .
> It is quite sufficient to focus your attention on a simple word . . . and without the intervention of analytical thought allow yourself to experience directly the reality it signifies. Do not use clever logic to examine or explain this word to yourself nor allow yourself to ponder its ramifications . . . I do not believe reasoning ever helps in the contemplative work.

As we recite our word one simply listens to the sound. We want to go beyond thoughts. Listening to it as a sound helps our concentration. We try to keep the body as still as possible. We are body, mind and spirit, and stillness of body will help to silence the mind. Of course there is a paradox here. Stillness of mind will also help keep the body still.

Meditation is simplicity itself. We hold ourselves alert and attentive during the entire time of prayer. As a fourth-century desert father put it, 'we centre ourselves, and focus on the God whom we do not see, whom we do not hear, but whose active presence we totally accept'. This is where faith enters into our prayer.

It is hard to believe that meditation is really as simple as it seems. We are tempted to complicate it. But meditation does get simpler as one goes along the path. Eventually as the mantra becomes rooted it will take less and less effort to say it as we enter into deeper and deeper realms of silence.

If we worry about what we are *feeling* during meditation we are courting discouragement. There is no such thing as a 'bad' meditation or a 'good' meditation. Be indifferent to what happens in the actual times of meditation. God does not judge us on how *well* we say the mantra but on our generosity, our faith, and our surrender to his indwelling presence. In meditation we want to come from the *head* to the *heart*.

We should not evaluate our progress in meditation. But be assured that meditation will gradually transform our lives into love if we persevere. Above all we should not evaluate our progress in what happens during the actual times of meditation. Sometimes we will be silent, sometimes we might be totally distracted. If you

THE 'HOW TO' OF MEDITATION

want to evaluate progress look to the inner transformation into love which is taking place in your daily life.

The most important thing about saying the mantra is to do it unhurriedly, calmly without any strain. Many newcomers find that as they meditate the mantra coincides with their breathing. This can tend to quiet the mind. But John Main with his Irish wit has the final word on breathing. He says 'at all costs continue to breathe for the entire time of your meditation'.

Meditation teaches us that *being* is more important than *doing*. The *heart* is more important than the *mind*. Our role is to be content with a loving, peaceful openness to God, without concern, without the desire to taste, or cling to, or possess God. We simply listen, watch and wait even though nothing seems to happen. In the Garden of Gethsemani Jesus says to his disciples 'could you not watch one hour with me?' In our daily periods of meditation we do watch this one hour with Jesus. In meditation we simply surrender ourselves and rest in God.

Meditation challenges us to overcome our self-centredness. Can we meditate without concern for where God is leading us? Can we meditate faithfully when distractions bombard us? Can we meditate when nothing 'happens' in meditation? Can we give up our desire to possess God and shed all desire for spiritual consolation in meditation?

The practice of daily meditation is also a spiritual discipline. The *Catechism of the Catholic Church* in talking about contemplative prayer states,

> The choice of the *time and duration of the prayer* arises from a determined will, revealing the secrets of the heart. One does not undertake contemplative prayer only when one has the time; one makes time for the Lord, with the firm determination not to give up, no matter what trials and dryness one may encounter . . . The heart is the place of this quest and encounter, in poverty and in faith. (2710)

In meditation faith, fidelity, commitment, perseverance and patience are the most important ingredients. We must be gentle with ourselves. We must try to let go and abandon ourself before the God whom we do not see, but whose presence we totally accept. We stand before the Lord and wait. As Father John never tired of saying: 'Meditation can be summed up in three words, say your mantra.'

In the Gospel the Lord speaks also about a mustard seed as a symbol of divine love. It is the smallest of all seeds, but grows into the tallest tree with its enormous capacity for growth. In meditation the repetition of the mantra, this small seed of divine love, has the power to grow within us and to transform us.

And finally meditation is a way of pure faith. Nothing else. We simply have to put this faith into practice each day.

4
The hunger for silence in prayer

Meditation is not the time for words, however beautifully and sincerely phrased. All our words are wholly ineffective when we come to enter into this deep and mysterious communion with God. In order to come into this holy and mysterious communion with the word of God indwelling within us, we must first have the courage to become more and more silent. In a deep, creative silence, we meet God in a way which transcends all our powers of intellect and language. We have to listen, to concentrate, to attend rather than to think.

Silence is really absolutely necessary for the human spirit if it really is to thrive, and not only just to thrive, but to be creative, to have a creative response to life, to our environment, to friends. Because the silence gives our spirit room to breathe, room to be. In silence, you don't have to be justifying yourself, apologising for yourself, trying to impress anyone. You just have to be, and it's a most marvellous experience when you come to it. And the wonder of it is in that experience, you are completely free. You are not trying to play any role, you are not trying to fulfill anyone's expectation.

(JOHN MAIN, *Word Into Silence*)

Great things seem to happen in silence. On that first Christmas Eve Jesus came to Mary, to the world and to us in the silence and stillness of the night. The divine office within the octave of the nativity says, 'while all things were in *quiet silence* and the night was in the midst of its course, your almighty word O Lord leapt down from your throne in heaven' (Wisdom 18:14–15). The most famous Christmas carol is called *Silent* Night. God *still* comes to us in the silence says John Main, but he comes to us now in the silence of our daily times of meditation.

We live in an age of frenetic activity. Television and radio programmes bombard us. We have wall-to-wall distractions at the end of the twentieth century. Anthropologists tell us we are cramming twice as much noise and activity into our lives as our ancestors. Our society is geared to activity, productivity, speed, material success and noise. We are losing the contemplative dimension of life, and we are paying the price. Noise is drowning out the voice of God. Like Jesus and the apostles, who often withdrew to a solitary place, we must also withdraw into the inner silence of our own soul. In this respect silence is both a psychological as well as a spiritual need.

John of the Cross in a letter to a Carmelite nun wrote: 'Our most important task consists in remaining silent before this great God ... He understands only one language that of silent love.' And another great spiritual teacher of India, Meher Baba (1895–1935) once said:

> A Mind that is fast is sick
> A Mind that is slow is sound
> A Mind that is still is divine.

This stillness was also so aptly described by the poet St John of the Cross when he wrote:

> One dark night,
> fired with love's urgent longings
> – oh the sheer grace! –
> I went out unseen,
> my house being now stilled.

Søren Kierkegaard (1813–54) the Danish philosopher echoed this need for silence when he wrote in *The Sickness unto Death*:

> The present state of the world and the whole of life is diseased. If I were a doctor and were asked for my advice, I should reply: Create Silence! Bring men to silence. The Word of God cannot be heard in the noisy world of today. And even if it were blazoned forth with all the panoply of noise so that it could be heard in the midst of all the other noise, then it would no longer be the Word of God. Therefore, create silence.

In the many times Jesus slipped away from the apostles, he would have spent the night in silent communication with his Father. We even find a reflection of this in human love. Two people in love often prefer to sit silently side by side, because talking would only disturb their loving union. Love unites with a bond that needs neither words or thoughts. That is what meditation is all about, and that is why silence is so important.

In *The World of Silence*, Max Picard (1888–1965) amplifies upon this point:

> The words of lovers increase the silence. They only serve to make the silence audible. Only love can increase the silence ... Lovers are conspirators of silence. When a man speaks to his

THE HUNGER FOR SILENCE IN PRAYER

beloved, she listens more to the silence than to the spoken words of her lover. 'Be silent', she seems to whisper. 'Be silent that I may hear . . .'

In meditation we go beyond thoughts, words, images into a deeper state of consciousness; we call this *silence*, a place where the Spirit actively works within us when the mind, senses and emotions have been quieted. The inner stillness and attentive listening in this silence is a total surrender to God in the depths of our being. Silence is the door that opens to the Kingdom of God within. But we need to be reminded that the silence of the heart is always a gift, a grace and cannot be won through exertion or will power on our part. All we can do is say our mantra with fidelity and perseverance and thus open ourselves to the possibility of receiving the gift of silence.

Perhaps John Main best summed up silence when he said, in one of his talks: 'You discover in the silence that you are loved, that you are lovable. It is the discovery everyone must make in their lives if they are going to become fully themselves, fully human.'

Abhishiktanada (Henri Le Saux) (1910–73), the French Benedictine who spent most of his life in India as a wandering Sannyasi (holy man), once wrote: 'People are on the lookout for ideas but I should like to make them feel that what they need is to keep silence. The Spirit only makes himself heard by those who humbly abide in silence.' And perhaps that great medieval Dominican, Meister Eckhart summed it up most succinctly when he said 'Nothing is so like God as silence'.

5
John Main, his life and teaching

Father John Main therefore embarks on his spiritual journey towards the mystery of God in its reality. Not by the futile effort of analysing and measuring what eternally eludes the grasp of our understanding, but by allowing himself to be totally immersed in the life of the Holy Trinity lived at the centre of his constantly expanding self.

It is in this sense that John Main was a Trinitarian Christian; in other words he was free of a created self that he had fully integrated and joyfully renounced to allow the self of God, the love relationship of the Holy Trinity, to rise at the centre of his consciousness. There he perfectly knew who he was. He was attentively present to himself because he was totally surrendered to the other, 'in whom', as St Paul says, 'we live, move and have our being' (Acts 17:28).

(FRANÇOIS C. GERARD (1924–91) in *John Main By Those Who Knew Him*)

The following capsule comments by Laurence Freeman on John Main's life are taken from the Introduction to my book *John Main by Those Who Knew Him*.

John Main was born in London, on 21 January 1926, the third child of David and Eileen Main. David Main, his father, was born in Ballinskelligs, County Kerry, Ireland. John Main's grandfather had moved there from Scotland as superintendent of the first transatlantic cable station. John Main loved Ballinskelligs, where some of the family still live. He felt it to be his *home*, a place where he belonged through blood and ancestral roots.

The Main home was a religious one of deep Catholic faith although Eileen Main had no hesitation in overlooking Friday abstinence from meat if it meant that good food was going to go bad. Waifs and strays, unwed mothers, abandoned wives or alcoholics were not only welcomed into the family, but often given the room of one of the family who would return to find themselves assigned to the living-room sofa.

John Main's early life included education with the Jesuits, as well as London's Westminster Cathedral Choir School, work as a journalist in London, wartime intelligence service with the Royal Corps of Signals in England and Belgium, a stint with a religious congregation, the Canons Regular, and finally a law degree at Trinity College, Dublin.

However, the next adventure in the direction of the East would change John Main's life and the lives of many of us for ever. He joined the British Colonial Service in 1954 and was assigned to Malaya. When he joined the British Colonial Service that autumn many countries in the British Empire were gaining their independence. John Main joined, eager to be involved in this momentous period of history.

He was assigned to Malaya and first studied Chinese in London at the School of Oriental and African Studies. He was to remember the motto inscribed over its front door when writing on meditation years later: the sign read 'knowledge is power'. John Main rejected that claim. He later wrote: 'the only *real* power is love'. But in 1954 he was eagerly absorbing new skills to train him for the job at hand.

One day in Kuala Lumpur he was sent on an apparently routine assignment to deliver a good-will message and a photograph to a Hindu monk, Swami Satyananda, director of an ashram and orphanage-school. John Main thought he would quickly dispatch the assignment and be free for the rest of the day. In fact this visit was to change his life and to set in motion a gradual understanding of his true vocation.

His good-will mission accomplished, John Main asked the swami to discuss the spiritual base of the many good works carried out at the orphanage and school. Within a few moments John Main knew he was in the presence of a holy man, a teacher, a man of the Spirit, whose faith was alive in love and service to others. As John Main subsequently wrote in *Christian Meditation, The Gethsemani Talks* many years later:

> I was deeply impressed by his peacefulness and calm wisdom, [and] he asked me if I meditated. I told him I tried to and, at his bidding, I described briefly what we have come to know as the Ignation method of discursive meditation; using the mind, memory and imagination. He was silent for a short time and then gently remarked that his own tradition of meditation was quite different. For the swami, the aim of meditation was the coming to awareness of the Spirit who dwells in our hearts . . . who enfolds the whole universe in his hands and in silence is loving to all.

This quotation from the swami is a passage from the ancient Indian scriptures – the Upanishads.

John Main was so moved by his intensity and devotion that he asked the swami to teach him to meditate his way. The swami agreed and invited him to come to a meditation centre once a week. On his first visit the swami spoke about how to meditate:

> To meditate you must become silent. You must be still and you must concentrate. In our tradition we know only one way in which you can arrive at that stillness, that concentration. We use a word that we call a mantra. To meditate, what you must do is to choose this word and then repeat it, faithfully, lovingly and continually. That is all there is to meditation. I really have nothing else to tell you. And now we will meditate.
>
> (*Christian Meditation, The Gethsemani Talks*)

However, the swami first pointed out that since the young Western visitor was a Christian, he must meditate with his Christian faith and he helped him choose a Christian mantra. He also insisted it was necessary to meditate twice a day, morning and evening. For eighteen months John Main meditated with the swami and it was this encounter that led John Main to the pilgrimage of meditation and eventually to discover the Christian tradition of the mantra in the practice of the early desert fathers.

After three years in Malaya, John Main returned to Ireland and Trinity College in 1956 to teach law. Then, in 1959 at age 33, John Main joined the Benedictine Abbey of Ealing in London, England.

Eleven years later, John Main accepted an invitation to become headmaster of St Anselm's Abbey School in Washington, DC. While at St Anselm's, he suggested one day to a sensitive young man that he read the book *Holy Wisdom* by a seventeenth-century Benedictine contemplative, Augustine Baker. The young man's response was so unexpectedly enthusiastic that John Main was moved to reread this spiritual classic. In this book he discovered the writings of a fourth-century desert monk – John Cassian. (See Chapter 8 on John Cassian.)

In the writings of Cassian, John Main found the link he had often wondered about. What Cassian had learned in the deserts of Egypt was what John Main had learned from a Hindu monk three years before becoming a Benedictine monk. What they both had in common was the teaching of the repetition of a word or short verse to bring one to an interior silence in prayer.

In 1974, John Main started his first Christian Meditation group at the Ealing Abbey Prayer Centre in London. Then, in 1977 at the invitation of Bishop Leonard Crowley of Montreal, John Main founded a Benedictine Monastery in Montreal dedicated to the teaching and the passing on of this tradition of Christian Meditation to others. This work has now become a 'monastery without walls' and is now carried on around the world by the World Community of Christian Meditation based in London. (See Chapter 21 on the role of the World Community for Christian Meditation.)

He had always felt he would not live to an old age. Father John died of cancer on the morning of 30 December 1982, radiating a sense of presence and peace and surrounded by his Benedictine monastic community and Montreal meditators. But his work was done. He had left a full teaching on meditation for future generations.

The influence of Skellig Michael

John Main's grandfather and indeed his father both worked with the first transatlantic cable station in Ballinskelligs, County Kerry, Ireland. He was deeply moved by the opening scene in the television programme *Civilization,* where Kenneth Clark opens the series on the Skellig rocks that rear up grandly from the Atlantic, seven miles off the coast of his beloved Ballinskelligs.

Ballinskelligs may have had a mysterious but hidden influence on John Main's future life. Irish monks built a monastic hermitage at the summit of Skellig Michael in the sixth century and monastic life continued there for over 600 years.

There is an intriguing conjecture concerning Skellig Michael. To Benedictine John Main is given much credit for recognising and rediscovering the teachings of John Cassian and the early Egyptian desert fathers on the use of a short phrase in prayer to bring one to an interior silence. St Benedict (480–550) was deeply influenced by Cassian's teachings. The writings of Cassian also played a decisive role in the life of John Main.

Cassian came to Provence in Gaul and brought a new influx of spiritual traditions from the desert fathers with the avowed aim of reforming Gallic monasticism. It was by way of Gaul and Cassian's monastery that monasticism spread to settlements such as Skellig Michael off the west coast of Ireland. *The New Catholic Encyclopedia* points out that 'by way of Gaul, particularly, was to be born the early Irish monasticism'.

Was the 'mantra' tradition of John Cassian and the desert fathers implanted on Skellig Michael from Gaul? Did John Main ever make this connection? Whether he did or not, it is an intriguing hypothesis that the teaching of the mantra came from the deserts of Egypt to Gaul to Ireland's Skellig Michael and that John Main, who spent part of his youth in sight of Skellig Michael, rediscovered in the twentieth century this ancient prayer tradition.

6
Scripture and meditation

Listen to Jesus' words in the Gospel of Matthew:

The Kingdom of heaven is like treasure lying buried in a field. The man who found it, buried it again; and for sheer joy went and sold everything he had, and bought that field.

Here is another picture of the Kingdom of heaven: a merchant, looking out for fine pearls, found one of very special value, so he went and sold everything he had and bought it.
(Matt. 13:44–6)

That's the sort of commitment that we need – the commitment to meditate everyday and, in our meditation, to say the mantra from the beginning to the end . . . There are no half measures. You can't decide to do a bit of meditation. The option is to meditate and to root your life in reality. As far as I can understand it, that is what the Gospel is about. That is what Christian prayer is about. A commitment to life, a commitment to eternal life. As Jesus himself put it, the Kingdom of heaven is here and now, what we have to do is to be open to it, which is to be committed to it.
(JOHN MAIN, *Moment of Christ*)

Both the Old and New Testaments are filled with passages that pertain to silence in prayer. John Main always laid great emphasis on anchoring this tradition of silence in Scripture.

The Old Testament speaks about finding God in silence. The psalmist (Ps. 46:10) says, 'Be still and know that I am God.' and Zachariah (2:13) says, 'Be silent everyone in the presence of the Lord.' There is also the beautiful story of the prophet Elijah. The Lord says to Elijah, 'Go outside and stand on the mountain; the Lord will be passing by.' A strong and heavy wind comes, but the Lord is not in the wind. There is a violent earthquake, but the Lord is not in the earthquake. Fire blazed up, but the Lord was not in the fire. Then came a gentle breeze and a still small voice and God speaks to Elijah in the silence (1 Kings 19:11-13).

Here are a few quotations and stories from the New Testament that have a bearing on the inner journey of Christian Meditation. As pointed out in Chapter 1 these are the words of Jesus from Luke 17 that are so pertinent to our journey of meditation: 'The Kingdom of God does not come in such a way as to be seen. No one will say "Look here it is," or "There it is," because the Kingdom of God is within you.' Christian Meditation is a daily pilgrimage to find the Kingdom within.

John Main often quoted the words of Jesus in Matthew (6:5-6)

And when you pray do not imitate the hypocrites; they love to say their prayers standing up in the synagogues and at the street corners for people to see them. I tell you solemnly they have had their reward. But when you pray go to your private room and, when you have closed the door, pray to your father who is in that secret place, and your father who sees all that is done in secret will reward you.

That secret place, says John Main, where we shut the door is our daily time of meditation and our own heart. That secret place is the deep centre of our being where God's activity is beyond our conscious perception. That secret place is the centre of our soul which we strive to reach through the daily spiritual discipline of meditation.

Father John also often repeated the words of Jesus (Matt. 6:7-8). 'In your prayer do not babble as the pagans do, for they think that by using many words they will make themselves heard. Do *not* be like them. Your Father knows what you need before you ask him.' This is another important aspect of meditation. God, all-knowing, all-seeing, knows our *real* needs much better than we know them ourselves. This means that all our petitions for ourselves and others can be brought silently before the Lord all in a matter of seconds as we begin our meditation.

In Mark's gospel (Mark 6:31) it is recorded that one day the apostles gathered around Jesus and reported to him all they had done and taught. Then, because there were so many people coming and going, Mark says 'they did not even have a chance to eat'. Jesus observing the frenzied activity, said to the twelve 'come with me by yourselves to a quiet place'. Mark continues that they went away by themselves in a boat to a solitary place. How many times in the gospels does Jesus withdraw to a solitary place?

This is the heart of meditation that we also have to withdraw each day from excessive noise and activity and find God in the solitary place of our own hearts.

Meditation also has much to do with a scene from the life of Jesus in the gospel of St Matthew (18:1–14)

> At this time the disciples came to Jesus and said, 'Who is the greatest in the Kingdom of heaven?' So he called a little child to him and sat the child in front of them. Then he said, 'I tell you solemnly, unless you change and become like little children you will never enter the kingdom of heaven. And so the one who makes himself as little as this child is the greatest in the kingdom of heaven.'

Learning to meditate is to become *childlike* but not childish. We have to leave adult complexity behind and to accept the simplicity of saying our sacred word with childlike faith. In meditation we give up our adult self-importance, and our adult self-centredness. We return each day to the childlike surrender of the mantra. We give up adult questions like 'is this doing me any good? Am I getting anywhere? How long is this going to take me?' On the contrary we must have the trust of a small child who accepts things with pure faith.

Finally, in relating meditation and Scripture, there is the gospel scene where Jesus visits the two sisters, Martha and Mary at Bethany. Martha is very busy and agitated and probably complains that Mary is not helping her. Jesus says, 'Martha, Martha, you are busy with many things but Mary has chosen the better part and it shall not be taken away from her' (Luke 10:41–42). And what was Mary doing? Mary was simply sitting in front of the Lord in silence. Exactly what we do in meditation. Martha was very busy probably getting lunch. Needless to say, biblical commentators have pointed out that if Martha had not been busy the three of them probably would not have eaten that day. But the point here is that there is a time for prayer and a time for getting lunch. I am sure that after Jesus left, Mary would have helped with the housework.

This is another reminder that we all have both a contemplative and an active dimension of life within us. There is no such thing as certain people who are 'contemplatives' and others who are 'actives'. We all combine the call to prayer and the call to fruitful action in our lives. But again let us not forget that Jesus said 'Mary has chosen the better part'.

7
The role of Mary on the contemplative journey

The essential Christian insight which Mary exemplifies in Luke's Gospel is poverty of spirit. This is purity of heart because it is unsullied by the intrusion of the egotistic will seeking for experience, desiring holiness, objectifying the Spirit or creating God in its own image. Mary reveals the basic simplicity of the Christian response in a poverty of spirit that consists in turning wholly to God, wholly away from self.

(JOHN MAIN, *The Other-Centredness of Mary*)

Mary is really the model and mother of the contemplative life for Christians because she *is* essentially described in the gospel as a person of prayer. As John Main once said, the secret of Mary's universal appeal in the twentieth century is her interiority and her other-centredness. He goes on to say, 'This is the essential Christian insight which Mary exemplifies in Luke's Gospel: Mary reveals the basic simplicity of the Christian response in a poverty of spirit that consists in turning wholly to God, wholly away from self.'

This poverty of spirit and turning away from self is, of course, the heart of our Christian Meditation practice. Like Mary we must continually seek to project our consciousness away from self. John Main points out that it was her other-centredness that makes Mary our model as meditators.

Christian Meditation is often referred to as 'Prayer of the Heart'. Mary's entire life was lived in her *heart*. St Luke mentions Mary's heart twice in his gospel. At the nativity Mary reflects on the words of the shepherds 'As for Mary, she treasured these things and pondered them in her *heart*' (Luke 2:19). At the finding of the child Jesus in the temple, 'His mother stored up all these things in her *heart*' (Luke 2:51). Mary knew the power of the Spirit at work in her heart. It is little wonder her life was one of contemplation.

Father Patrick Eastman, editor of the spiritual journal *Monos*, comments that in her *surrender* at the Annunciation,

Mary is still and silent, she hears the spoken word and gives consent for that spoken word to be enfleshed within her and God breathes upon her and it is done. The word is made flesh and comes to bring healing into a broken world and the Church as Body of Christ is born. Now let us move to our times of prayer. Is not the same process at work? We are invited by God's grace to be still and silent that we may hear the word spoken to us. Prayer then becomes a silence and stillness where we surrender to God.

Mary is often termed the 'listening heart of Israel' and 'the woman wrapped in silence'. But to listen does require silence. In her listening, Mary's silence was one of deep joy as she rejoiced in God her saviour (Luke 1:47).

In our final view of Mary in the Acts of the Apostles we see her still at prayer with the apostles in the upper room in Jerusalem, waiting for the coming of the Spirit (1:14). Perhaps that is ultimately her role with those who meditate: to bring that Spirit to us in the silence; to give birth to Jesus in our hearts. Our role in meditation is to wait in silence and faith for the utterance of his word within us.

Mary's famous *fiat*, 'Let it be done unto me according to your word' (Luke 1:38) is the same *fiat* we must express on the path of Christian Meditation. In meditation we must be open to whatever happens, whether it is the sense of God's presence or absence, distractions or silence, everything must be totally accepted in the spirit of Mary's fiat.

8
The historical roots of silence in prayer

Throughout Christian history, men and women of prayer have fulfilled a special mission in bringing their contemporaries, and even succeeding generations, to the same enlightenment, the same rebirth in Spirit that Jesus preached.

One of these teachers was John Cassian, in the fourth century, who has a claim to be one of the most influential teachers of the spiritual life in the West. His special importance as the teacher and inspirer of St. Benedict and so of the whole of Western monasticism, derives from the part he played in bringing the spiritual tradition of the East into the living experience of the West.

(JOHN MAIN, *Letters from the Heart*)

Cassian recommended anyone who wanted to learn to pray continually to take a single short verse and to repeat this verse over and over again. In his Tenth Conference (10:10) he urges this method of simple and constant repetition as the best way of casting out all distractions and monkey chatter from our mind, in order for it to rest in God.

(JOHN MAIN, *Word Into Silence*)

John Cassian, the desert fathers and the hesychast tradition of prayer

The word 'hesychast' is a derivative of a Greek word meaning tranquillity or peace. It has its roots in the spiritual tradition of the fourth-century hermits who settled in the deserts of Syria and particularly Egypt. It was essentially a contemplative tradition based on continuous prayer and emphasis on the indwelling presence of Christ. These early desert monks employed a *formula* of reciting a short biblical verse to come to an interior silence in prayer. Today we would equate the *formula* with a *mantra*. We are indebted to John Cassian and his monk companion Germanus for describing this prayer practice of the desert monks.

John Cassian was born in the year AD 360 in what today is

THE HISTORICAL ROOTS OF SILENCE IN PRAYER

Croatia. He learned both Latin and Greek, became a monk and travelled to Egypt to visit the desert fathers. He spent the last years of his life in what today is Marseilles, France, where he founded a double monastery. In Marseilles his local bishop and fellow monks urged him to talk about his years in Egypt, what it was like, what he was taught, what he had experienced. Eventually Cassian recorded all that he had learned on prayer in his famous Tenth Conference on prayer. The great English Benedictine scholar Abbot Cuthbert Butler said it is a treatise on prayer that has never been surpassed. The conference is available in a book entitled 'John Cassian' in the series *The Classics of Western Spirituality*.

In this Tenth Conference Cassian gives a lengthy account of a conversation between Germanus and himself as pupils and a great spiritual leader in the desert, Abba Isaac, as teacher.

On their first visit Abba Isaac had told them that those who prayed must keep their minds in silence and stillness. On their second visit, having *tried* to pray in silence, Germanus put their problem to Isaac. They wanted to pray like this, he said, but they found that their minds went travelling far and wide, from one idea or image to another, from one distraction to another. Germanus said 'I believe this happens because we haven't got any point to focus on. We need something to stop the wandering of our thoughts.'

On hearing this Isaac was happy. Such an insight, he said, showed that the two young men were half-way to the solution. 'With God's guidance,' he said, 'I think it will be easy to bring you to the heart of true prayer.' Then he taught them to pray by means of a mantra or prayer verse or what Cassian in the Latin of his day called a 'formula'. He urged them to repeat a verse of Psalm 70 'come to my help, O God; Lord hurry to my rescue'. He also urged them to say this verse over and over until it became rooted in their very being. They should go on repeating this verse, said Isaac, 'Until it casts away the multiplicity of other thoughts'. 'Restrict yourself', said Isaac, 'to the *poverty* of this simple verse, and reject all the abundant riches of thought and words. This verse must always be in your heart.'

Isaac tied in the poverty of this simple verse to the beatitude 'Blessed are the poor in spirit for theirs is the Kingdom of heaven' (Matt. 6:3). Isaac also told Cassian and Germanus to repeat this verse both in prosperity and adversity. This is where we get the tradition of the continuous recitation of the mantra in our daily times of meditation.

John Cassian brought this teaching on prayer into Western Europe. Cassian was also the spiritual teacher of St Benedict. Benedict urged that Cassian be read regularly in the monasteries of his rule. It was through Benedictine communities that Cassian's teaching on prayer spread to the West. The Rule of St Benedict points out that prayer in community should be marked by its brevity.

In the East this form of prayer went from the deserts of Egypt to Greece, Slavonic lands and particularly to Russia where the 'Jesus' mantra took deep roots. The book *The Way of the Pilgrim* has become a Russian spiritual classic and outlines the saying of the formula by a Russian peasant who travels through that land. The Jesus Prayer developed from the formula and is widely practised on Mount Athos, an island of Orthodox monasteries situated off the coast of Greece. The Jesus Prayer in fact has become the foundation of Eastern Orthodox spirituality.

However, John Main suggested an alternative mantra to a biblical phrase with the name Jesus for a very important reason. For Western head-centred people, suggested Father John, the word 'Jesus' can immediately start us to picturing Christ, limiting our relationship to Him to merely thinking about Christ. But in meditation we are attempting to enter a silence, beyond thinking about Jesus; a silence where our union with Jesus can be fully realised. This is why Father John recommended the mantra *maranatha* in Aramaic, a language that would not conjure up any thoughts or images. However it should be noted that *maranatha* in English means 'Come Lord (Jesus)' so again we have a tie in to the ancient tradition of the Jesus prayer. Those who practice the Jesus mantra, especially members of the Orthodox Church, would generally deny any problem with the Jesus Prayer being in their own language, pointing out that its simple recitation does indeed lead to silence.

Cassian does describe, in Christian terms and with scriptural support, a *universal* spiritual discipline that leads to unity and integration of all levels of consciousness. The tradition is reflected in this *hesychastic* school which teaches the unity of mind and heart in the practice of silent prayer. The continual recitation of the mantra roots the verse or word in the heart, thus gradually leading to the state of continuous prayer enjoined by Christ (Luke 18:1) and by St Paul (1 Thess 5:17). By leaving behind 'the riches of thought and imagination' (Cassian) the mantra leads to poverty of spirit, the condition of letting go, of radical non-possessiveness which applies eventually not only to what we have or what we do but even to what we are: the Lord's command to his disciples to 'leave self behind' and all one's possessions (Luke 9:23; 14:33).

It can be seen from the practice of the 'formula', now called the Jesus Prayer that the practice of Christian Meditation came from the same spiritual roots and the same desert tradition. The tradition of the 'formula', or the Jesus mantra and the mantra maranatha came out of the same way of silent, unceasing prayer practised by the early desert monks. All mantras are repeated to keep the mind and heart attentive to God's presence. The Jesus Prayer is centred in the heart.

Bishop Theophane the Recluse (1815–94) said 'in prayer the principal thing is to stand before him unceasingly day and night until the end of life.' John Main recommends that the mantra 'maranatha' be sounded and rooted in the heart. Both practices lay stress on the important involvement of the whole person, body, mind and spirit.

Those who practice the Jesus Prayer say it has the power to restore harmony and unity through integration of mind and heart. John Main says the mantra maranatha has the same integrating power. In the book *Word Into Silence* he says the mantra 'is like a harmonic that we sound in the depth of our spirit, bringing us to an ever deepening sense of our own wholeness and central harmony.'

In all essential aspects, with the exception of the mantra itself, the similarities between Cassian's 'formula', the Jesus Prayer and the 'mantra' of John Main are expressions of the deeper practice of prayer in the Christian tradition.

The English connection: *The Cloud of Unknowing*

The anonymous English spiritual classic *The Cloud of Unknowing* is important because we see continuity in the teaching on silent prayer of John Cassian (fourth century), the *Cloud of Unknowing* (fourteenth century) and John Main (twentieth century). All three teachers offer the same essential teaching.

The central theme of *The Cloud* is that God cannot be reached by the human intellect but only by a silent prayer of love that can pierce 'the cloud of unknowing'. The author of this book says that God hides in the cloud of unknowing. He takes this image from the book of Exodus where the Israelites are led through the desert, a cloud by day and a pillar of fire by night. Also at the transfiguration God appears in a cloud and says 'this is my beloved son' (2 Peter 1:16–18).

The author of *The Cloud* talks very clearly about the use of a mantra which can be used to pierce this cloud of unknowing where God hides. He says 'we must pray in the height, depth, length and breath of our spirit, not in many words but in a *little* word. And he urges us to set aside our thoughts, words and imagination and consign everything to what he calls the 'cloud of forgetting'. He says we must give up all our thoughts and ideas of God, for 'God can be touched, embraced and loved, but *not* by thought'. *The Cloud* says this about the use of a mantra in prayer:

> Take a short word, preferably of one syllable . . . the shorter the word the better. A word like God or love. Choose which you like, or perhaps some other, so long as it is of one syllable. And fix this word fast to your heart, so that it is always there come what may. This short word pierces heaven. This word is to be your shield and your spear, whether in peace or in war, with this word beat upon the cloud.
>
> Lift up your heart to God with humble love: desire God but not what you can get out of him. Don't think of anything so that nothing occupies your mind or will but only God. Try to forget all created things. Let them go and pay no attention to them. Do not give up but work away. When you begin you find only darkness and a cloud of unknowing. Reconcile yourself to wait in this darkness as long as is necessary, but go on longing after him you love. Strike that thick cloud of unknowing with your word, that dart of longing love, and on no account think of giving up. You are to reach out with a naked intention directed towards God and him alone.

Here are some other points the author of *The Cloud* makes about this prayer of repeating a short word, the prayer of seeking God in silence and stillness.

- He warns us that we should come to prayer with no expectations, not seeking to receive any special experiences, visions, to hear voices and so on. *The Cloud* says that essential union with God is beyond all experiences.
- *The Cloud* says one must empty the mind of all images and thoughts and simply rest in darkness, in the darkness of the cloud of unknowing. The author says that out of this darkness of faith will come a stirring of ardent love. The purpose of emptying the mind of images and concepts, says *The Cloud*, is to make one capable of receiving God's gift of love. He emphasizes that human conceptual knowledge is totally inadequate and imperfect. God, he says, is beyond anything we can imagine.
- The author of *The Cloud* writes that this way of silent prayer is simplicity itself and that even the most unlearned person can attain to this silence. He says this spiritual discipline is uncomplicated, and simply a normal development of the ordinary Christian life. Two other great medieval spiritual teachers, Meister Eckhart (1260–1327) and Johannes Tauler

(1300–1361) reflect a similar teaching that the heights of contemplative prayer are offered to ordinary people.
- *The Cloud* stresses that God does the main work in this prayer. Our work, says the author, is to become silent but even this cannot be done without the help of grace. To be silent in prayer, he says, far from being a mere technique, is in fact a distinct call from God.
- Another point *The Cloud* makes is that we should not be carried away by superficial feelings of any kind, be they feelings of joy or sadness, elation or depression. The author says in this prayer remain poised at a deep point of recollection and in the ground of your being. Even Satan, he says, cannot enter this inner chamber of your heart in this prayer. In this silence one can only be open to the voice of the Spirit.
- *The Cloud* insists that by remaining silent in prayer, we are in fact helping the whole human race. While we do not think explicitly of anybody, we in fact are helping everybody.
- *The Cloud* points out that this prayer burns out the roots of sin and performs a function that *cannot* be accomplished by fasting, self-denial or self-inflicted penances. This flame of love that burns in prayer, says *The Cloud*, penetrates to a level of the personality upon which these penances and practices have no effect.
- *The Cloud* even inserts a little bit of humour. Perhaps with tongue in cheek the author says contemplative silence even changes one's appearance, giving serenity to one's demeanour, unifying the personality and making one attractive to others. He says 'even those who are not highly endowed by nature are rendered beautiful by this prayer'. Unfortunately, he does not say anything about losing weight or wrinkles disappearing.
- *The Cloud* also talks about the cost involved in this prayer. The author says 'it is hard work, very hard work indeed'.

One can see the great influence the *Cloud of Unknowing* had on the prayer teaching of John Main. *The Cloud* is still one of the great spiritual classics of our time. It is available in a paperback edition with an introduction by the Jesuit William Johnston. Another recommended book is the *Mysticism of the Cloud of Unknowing* by the same William Johnston.

A continuous tradition

Every age has its Christian contemplatives, teachers and leaders from various countries and cultures emphasising contemplative silence in prayer.

In the deserts of Egypt to the tenth century in addition to Cassian there is Abba Isaac, Evagrius, Origen, St Augustine, St Gregory the Great, St John Climacus, St John Chrysostom, John Scotus Erigena, Symeon the New Theologian, Dionysius the Areopagite, Clement of Alexandria, and St Gregory of Nyssa.

In the Middle Ages and between the tenth and fourteenth centuries we have St Bernard of Clairvaux, St Bonaventure, St Thomas Aquinas, St Francis of Assissi, William of St Thierry, Hugh of St Victor, Gregory Palamas, Meister Eckhart and the Rhineland mystics, Ruysbroeck, Suso and Tauler.

In the fourteenth century there is the author of the *Cloud of Unknowing*, Walter Hilton, Catherine of Siena and Julian of Norwich; in the fifteenth century Nicholas of Cusa; in the sixteenth century the Spanish Carmelites St John of the Cross and St Teresa of Avila.

From the sixteenth to the nineteenth centuries Theophane the Recluse, St Francis de Sales, Blaise Pascal, Jean-Pierre de Caussade, the author of *The Way of the Pilgrim*, William Law, St Jane de Chantal, St Thérèse of Lisieux and Brother Lawrence.

In the twentieth century we have had a wide range of contemplatives, spiritual leaders and teachers writing on the importance of silence in prayer including six Benedictines, Dom Augustine Baker, Dom John Chapman, Swami Abhishiktananda (Henri Le Saux), Bede Griffiths, John Main and Laurence Freeman; also Thomas Merton, Bernard Lonergan, Teilhard de Chardin, Charles Peguy, Edith Stein, William James, Kallistos Ware, Simone Weil, Etty Hillesum, Charles de Foucauld, Evelyn Underhill, Karl Rahner, Jacques and Raissa Maritain, Etienne Gilson, Friedrich von Hügel, Mother Teresa, Jean Vanier, Thomas Keating, Basil Pennington, George Maloney, William Johnston and a host of others.

9
The universal call to contemplative prayer

There is no greater need in the Church and in the world today than for the renewed understanding that the call to prayer, to deep prayer, in universal.

(JOHN MAIN, Word Into Silence)

All growth that endures in nature must be thoroughly rooted, and it is the summons of each one of us to be thoroughly rooted in Christ. I think there is a real sense in which meditation is a return to our original innocence. The Fathers describe this way as 'purity of heart'. The call of each one of us from Jesus is to find it unclouded by egoism, unclouded by images, unclouded by desire.

Meditation leads us to the clarity that comes from original and eternal simplicity. So we are content simply to be with him, content simply and in a childlike way to say our word, our one word, from the beginning to the end of our meditation.

To begin to meditate requires nothing more than the determination to begin. To begin to discover our roots, to begin to discover our potential, to begin to return to our source. And God is our source. In the simplicity of meditation beyond all thought and imagination we begin to discover in utter simplicity that we are in God; we begin to understand that we are in God in whom we live and move and have our being. We try to describe this growing awareness that we discover in the silence and daily commitment as 'undivided consciousness'.

Meditation is just this state of simplicity that is the fully mature development of our original innocence ... The wonder of the proclamation of Christianity is that everyone of us is invited into this same state of simple, loving union with God. This is what Jesus came both to proclaim and to achieve. This is what each of us is invited to be open to.

(JOHN MAIN, Moment of Christ)

A call to all or just a chosen few?

One question that arises on the meditation path is whether contemplative prayer is a call to everyone. When the psalmist said 'be still and know that I am God' did he in fact express this as an insight for everyone?

Thomas Merton (1915–68), the great American Cistercian monk and writer, was adamant that the fall from paradise in Genesis was a fall from the contemplative state and a loss of the original unity with God. As William Shannon points out in *Thomas Merton's Dark Path*:

> Contemplation is also the key to Merton's understanding of redemption. Redemption is the return to the paradisal state. It is the recovery of the original unity that characterized the human condition as God intended and intends us to be. It is the overcoming of all that alienates us from God, from our own true selves, and from our fellow human beings. The way back to paradise and to original unity is the road to contemplation.

Merton came to realise that contemplation was not an esoteric call but a universal call to everyone because of our basic humanity. And he also understood the contemplative call for Christians to arise from our baptism. His great feeling for the contemplative calling was expressed in a poem from *The Tears of the Blind Lions*.

> May my bones burn and ravens eat my flesh
> If I forget thee, contemplation.

In *What is Contemplation* Merton writes:

> The seeds of contemplation are planted in every Christian soul at Baptism. But seeds must grow and develop before you reap the harvest. There are thousands of Christians walking about the face of the earth bearing in their bodies the infinite God of whom they know practically nothing. The seeds of contemplation have been planted in these souls, but they merely lie dormant. They do not germinate.

Everywhere men and women are looking for greater interiority in their lives. A few years ago in Australia I was introduced by the Anglican rector of a cathedral when he said 'Mr Harris will speak on Christian Meditation, the best kept secret in the Church today'. That is the greatest challenge of the spiritual life today: to share the teaching of Christian Meditation with others so that the seeds of contemplation will germinate in men and women everywhere. As the *Catechism of the Catholic Church* says, 'the living and true God tirelessly calls each person to that mysterious encounter known as

THE UNIVERSAL CALL TO CONTEMPLATIVE PRAYER 37

prayer' (2567). And the psalmist says, 'If today you hear his voice, harden not your hearts' (Psalm 95:8).

Regarding those who never hear the contemplative call, Thomas Merton elaborates on the gospel story of the sower who scatters the seeds; some seeds fall in the path and are eaten up by the birds of the air, other seeds fall in shallow ground, do not take root, wither and die, but other seeds fall on fertile ground and bear fruit in due season. Merton points out that excessive activity, cares and concerns of the world often drown out the voice of God calling us to this way of prayer. In our excessive busyness, the seeds, (God's call) are eaten up by the birds of the air or fall on infertile ground.

Some people drop out of the daily practice of silent prayer because they have brought to meditation too many impatient expectations. They are looking for 'instant results'. They have still to learn how to meditate and 'to let go and let God'. Others find the daily spiritual discipline too great a demand. Whatever the reason, people who give up should never feel self-rejective about it. God often writes straight with crooked lines. Perhaps at a more propitious time in their lives they will return to the practice. Grace works in mysterious ways. To those who drop out, those who carry on should offer a continuing friendship, love and support, and leave everything else in the hands of the Lord.

The second hit on the head

It is well to remember that Jesus takes the initiative in deepening our prayer and it is Jesus who issues the invitation. Many people who are now meditating talk in fact about a *double* invitation. There often seems to be two knocks at the door: 'Behold I stand at the door and knock.'

It was June Longworth, an Air Canada flight attendant and a member of the United Church of Canada who first coined the phrase getting 'hit on the head twice' about the call of God to meditation. June was first hit on the head at a dinner party where she happened upon a conversation about Christian Meditation and a Benedictine monk named John Main. Cautious at first, she nevertheless managed to locate some of John Main's books and was introduced to the teaching through *Word Into Silence*.

Subsequently she was flying from Toronto to London and received her second 'hit on the head'. In a seat next to her work station she noticed a passenger reading a book, the biography of John Main *In the Stillness Dancing*. The passenger was Father Jim Dempsey, an Irish priest working in Canada. Father Jim and June discovered they lived only a short distance from each other near

Cambridge, Ontario. He invited her to join his meditation group, which she did. June says that after two hits on the head and particularly John Main's liberal use of Scripture, she suddenly came to a realisation that this was the prayer, discipline and spiritual life she had always longed for. June was a recipient of a *double* invitation.

Perhaps one of the most dramatic stories of this double invitation is told by Brigette Ahlften, a young teacher in Berlin, Germany. Following a retreat weekend in Bavaria she visited the monastery book store. She says she walked directly to a shelf of about 200 books and for no *apparent* reason chose to buy one book, perhaps because of the brilliant red cover. That book was John Main's *Word Into Silence*, translated into German. She had no time to read the book because the following week she was on her holidays, bicycling in Ireland with a girl friend. At a stop in Dublin she overheard a person mention the name of John Main and a meditation group meeting to be held that day. She attended the meeting. Thus was Brigette launched on the path with her second knock on the door, her second invitation.

It would seem that for some people God does issue a double invitation to this path of Christian Meditation. And Thomas Merton put it so well: 'we become contemplatives when God discovers Himself in us.' We must always remember that the call to meditation is a gift and a grace from God: 'If today you hear his voice, harden not your hearts' (Psalm 95:8).

The first shall be last and the last shall be first

Remember the Lord's mysterious statement 'the first shall be last and the last shall be first' (Mark 10:31). These words of Jesus can certainly be applied to the many wounded and broken people who are given the gift of meditation at 'the last hour', so to speak. Time and time again we see people come to meditation at a time of trauma or crisis in their lives. People who are dying often seem to be given the gift of meditation to assist them in their preparation for death. Many people in Alcoholics Anonymous (AA) follow up on step eleven of their twelve-stop programme which urges them to prayer and meditation.

It should not be surprising to us that the author of *The Cloud of Unknowing* speaks very prophetically about this. Six hundred years ago in the fourteenth century *The Cloud* spoke about God's generosity with this gift of silence. The author of *The Cloud* says:

> I believe too our Lord deliberately chooses to work in those

THE UNIVERSAL CALL TO CONTEMPLATIVE PRAYER 39

who have been habitual sinners rather than in those who by comparison, have never grieved him at all. Yes he seems to do this very often. For I think he wants us to realize that he is all merciful and almighty, and that he is perfectly free to work as he pleases, where he pleases, and when he pleases.

We do not use the term habitual sinners any more, but the reference is very clear. God *often* gives the gift of silent prayer to those who have reached rock-bottom in their lives. A concrete example of this, fulfilling *The Cloud*'s insight, is the story of Galilee House in Ireland. (See Chapter 17 on the healing aspects of Christian Meditation and the path from brokenness to wholeness.)

10
The mantra/prayer word and its role in Christian Meditation

Time and again the practical advice of masters of prayer is summed up in the simple injunction: 'Say your mantra'; 'Use this little word'. The Cloud of Unknowing *advises, 'and pray not in many words but in a little word of one syllable. Fix this word fast to your heart so that it is always there come what may. With this word you will suppress all thoughts.'*

Abbot Chapman, in his famous letter of Michaelmas 1920 from Downside, describes the simple, faithful use of a mantra which he had discovered more from his own courageous perseverance in prayer than from teachers. He had rediscovered a simple enduring tradition of prayer that entered the West through Monasticism, and first entered Western Monasticism through John Cassian in the late fourth century. Cassian himself received it from the holy men of the desert who placed its origin back beyond living memory to Apostolic times.

The venerable tradition of the mantra in Christian prayer is above all attributable to its utter simplicity. It answers all the requirements of the masters' advice on how to pray because it leads us to a harmonious, attentive stillness of mind, body and spirit. It requires no special talent or gift apart from serious intent and the courage to persevere. 'No one', Cassian said, 'is kept away from purity of heart by not being able to read nor is rustic simplicity any obstacle to it for it lies close at hand for all if only they will by constant repetition of this phrase keep the mind and heart attentive to God.'

Our mantra is the ancient Aramaic prayer, 'Maranatha, Maranatha', 'Come Lord. Come Lord Jesus.'

(JOHN MAIN, *Word Into Silence*)

John Cassian, the fourth century desert monk, called it a *formula*. John Main often calls it a *prayer word*. Contemporary usage has popularised the word *mantra*.

Eknath Easwaran in *Meditation – Commonsense Directions for an Uncommon Life* points out that the two-syllable word 'mantra' comes from the Sanscrit words *man* 'the mind' and *tri* 'to cross'. The

THE MANTRA/PRAYER WORD AND ITS ROLE

mantra practised as a spiritual discipline enables us to cross the sea of the mind. The sea, says Easwaran, is another apt image for the mind. Ever changing, the sea is calm one day and turbulent the next. Our minds are drifting about on the surface, blown by every distraction on the treacherous waters. We can never make the crossing without some help. That is the role of the mantra.

In fact to use another figure of speech what the mantra eventually does is take us down to the bottom of the sea, where everything is calm and tranquil. On the surface there may be crashing waves (our mind, our distractions) but at the bottom of the sea it is always quiet and our hearts are calm and silent.

A mantra is simply a sacred word or a phrase which is repeated continuously at our times of meditation to bring us to an interior silence in the presence of the Lord. The aim of the mantra is to bring us to our own centre, our own heart where we learn to be awake, alive and open to the indwelling Spirit. In this stillness and peace we not only become aware of God's presence but we *experience* this presence.

In that great nineteenth-century Russian spiritual classic *The Way of a Pilgrim*, the Russian peasant/author says this about the repetition of a mantra:

> Many so-called enlightened people regard this frequent offering of one and the same prayer as useless and even trifling, calling it mechanical and a thoughtless occupation of simple people. But unfortunately they do not know how this frequent service of the lips imperceptibly becomes a genuine appeal of the heart, sinks down into the inner life, becomes a delight, becomes as it were, natural to the soul, bringing it light and nourishment and leading it on to union with God.

The aim of repeating a word in our meditation periods is to lead us away from thoughts, ideas, images and open us to the prayer of Jesus within us. John Main says 'By means of the mantra we leave behind all passing images and learn to rest in the infinity of God himself.'

The mantra leads us to inner stillness beyond distraction and the self-centred consciousness of the ego. *The Cloud of Unknowing* says 'Fix the word in your mind so that it will be there come what may' (see Chapter 8 on *The Cloud*). For John Main, the power of the mantra lies in its simplicity. He advises the repetition of the word until the person can no longer say it because to *choose* to stop saying it would be to return to the dualistic level of prayer in which the ego once again is observing, choosing and controlling.

At times the mantra may lead into complete silence. Once we

have become conscious of the silence in a way that could be expressed as 'I am silent', we are no longer silent and need, therefore, to return to the purifying work of the mantra. The mantra is the way of *kenosis*, an emptying of egoism that leads to 'fullness of being, the fullness of God himself' (Eph. 3:19).

John Main in speaking about the integrating power of the mantra says:

> The faithful repetition of the word integrates our whole being. It does so because it brings us to the silence, the concentration, the necessary level of consciousness that enables us to open our mind and heart to the work of the love of God in the depth of our being.
>
> (*Moment of Christ*)

The mantra is a spiritual discipline, a help towards concentration, enabling us to go beyond words, thoughts, even holy thoughts. It is also a daily discipline and a labour we have to accept. We say the mantra slowly, steadily with attentiveness. When we find our mind has wandered we simply come back to our mantra. There is therefore nothing secret or magical about the mantra. It is simply a daily calling upon God, a spiritual discipline of *love*.

John Main tells us that if we persevere on the path of meditation gradually the mantra begins to take root. It begins as it were to sound in the heart and we begin to hear the mantra at a much deeper level of our being. The mantra he says should be said unhurriedly and calmly but we must be humble and we must be patient. The mantra says to God 'I am open to your presence, I am resting in your presence, I am in your hands. Do whatever you will with me.' The mantra is our surrender to God.

But John Main reminds us that we cannot attempt to force the pace of meditation. We must let go of goals and trying to achieve anything. The mantra will become rooted in our consciousness through the simple fidelity of returning to the mantra each morning and each evening. In perseverance we will stand with the mind in the heart before God.

If we start asking questions like 'how far have I come' or 'how long is all of this going to take me' or 'am I becoming holier' then we are becoming self-conscious, something we want to avoid. Meditation, says Father John, requires simplicity and we are led to that simplicity by faithfully saying the mantra.

Another great secret of the mantra is that it prevents us from getting stuck either in the past or in the future. So many of us waste our time analysing or living in the past or fantasising about the future, all of which is a waste of time. What is vital is to live in the *present* moment, the only moment in time that is important.

And the great secret of saying our mantra is that it *can* bring us into this present moment.

When we say our mantra we cannot be thinking of the past or the future. We are inserted in the *now*. If we read the letters of St Paul we realise Paul was always living in the present moment. He says '*now* is the hour of salvation, *now* is the acceptable time, *now* is the time to rise from sleep.' Not yesterday, not tomorrow, but *now*. The continuous recitation of the mantra does bring us into the present moment.

The mantra should be repeated silently with as much attention as we are capable of giving. The mantra will then descend to the deepest level of consciousness until it becomes as natural as breathing. Again, we listen to the mantra as a sound. Listening to it as a sound helps our concentration to move from thought to being.

It is hard to believe that meditation and saying our mantra is really as simple as it seems. We are tempted to complicate it. But meditation does get simpler as we persevere on the path. In the beginning we say the mantra at the surface level of our mind but eventually as the mantra becomes rooted it will take less and less effort to recite it. Our work is simply to say it with faith, love and openness to God's presence. This constant daily practice will indeed root the mantra deep in our consciousness. It will become our friend and companion.

Finally, however, we should always remember that the way of the mantra is not a technique or a method for accomplishing some goal . . . even the goal of silence. Silence only points the finger towards God. The discipline of meditation requires faith, trust, letting go, openness, attention, joy and most important of all *love*. Everything else we leave in the hands of the Lord.

Choosing the mantra

As previously mentioned, maranatha is one of the oldest Christian prayers. It is a word in Aramaic, the language that Jesus spoke, and means 'Come Lord Jesus' or 'The Lord Comes'. St Paul ends his first letter to the Corinthians with this word and it is the last word in St John's book of Revelation (1 Cor. 16:22; Rev. 22:20). Paul was writing to the Corinthians in Greek but at the end of his letter inserts the Aramaic word *maranatha*. Scripture scholars tell us Paul was able to do this because all the early Christians fully understood this word. It was a password which allowed Christians into homes for the celebration of the Eucharist.

Maranatha also appears in one of the oldest written liturgical fragments of the Eucharist that exists. In the invitation to receive communion the priest says:

> Praise to the Son of David. If anyone is holy, let them come. If anyone is not holy, let them repent. Maranatha. Come Lord Jesus.
>
> (*Didache* 10)

While maranatha is a sacred word to Christians, nevertheless at our times of meditation one does not dwell on the meaning of the word. One wants to go beyond thoughts and images and simply rest in silence in the Lord. A mantra is not something that is magical or mysterious. It is really something very practical since it calms our minds and hearts and brings us into the presence of God.

Again, in reciting Maranatha the word is broken into four equal stressed syllables ma-ra-na-tha. And one listens to the word as a sound as it is said gently, continuously for the full period of meditation. John Main says there may come the day when we enter the cloud of unknowing, in which there is silence, absolute silence, and we can no longer hear the mantra. This absolute silence may last for only a short period of time and then we must return to saying the mantra.

Other Christian mantras

John Main mentions the word Jesus used in his own prayer, 'Abba'. Like maranatha this word is also in Aramaic and means 'Father'. John Main also mentions the name Jesus, although he felt the Jesus mantra had certain difficulties for some head-centred Westerners. (See Chapter 8 on the Jesus Prayer.)

The author of the *Cloud of Unknowing* felt there was importance in choosing a short word of one syllable. Maranatha ties into this since it is actually four equally stressed syllables when it is recited slowly in conjunction with our breathing.

The choice of a mantra is an important one and ideally should be sanctified by long usage. A mantra is also generally handed down by a teacher, such as John Main, considered by many Christian meditators around the world as their teacher.

Bearing in mind the aforementioned points about choosing a mantra, here are a few mantras for Christians suggested by a variety of spiritual writers. Notice that many of them depart from the tradition of *The Cloud* and John Main of a one syllable or four equally stressed syllable mantras: Abba, Peace, Come Holy Spirit, Kyrie Eleison, Christ is Risen, my Lord and my God, Veni Sancti Spiritus, O Lord Make Haste to Help me, God is love.

Changing one's mantra

Because we want the mantra to become rooted within us, the traditional teaching is to choose one mantra and stay with it. If we continually transplant a plant and uproot it several times, there may come a time when the roots having been disturbed simply do not root again. Some people when they come into a difficult time with distractions in their meditation, feel it is time to change their mantra. It is part of the restlessness of our age. Try one mantra for six weeks and then another. It simply does not work that way. Choose one mantra, stick with it and let it become rooted deep within you.

There is a lovely story (apocryphal) about an old desert hermit with a mantra that had been rooted within him for 40 years. Sometimes he liked to recite it out loud. His deep life of meditation enabled him to work minor miracles like calling down the rain from the sky, walking on water on a nearby river, and other neat things, or so the story goes. One day some visiting monks heard him chanting his mantra and felt he was not pronouncing his word correctly. So they decided fraternal correction was in order and they taught him how to pronounce it the correct way. The hermit was humble and thanked them profusely for the correct pronunciation. From that point on he said it correctly. However the next time he went to walk on water he sank to the bottom of the river.

The Hindu meditation teacher Eknath Easwaran relates the story of Sri Ramakrishna who once compared a person who keeps changing the mantra to a farmer who digs in ten different places looking for water. The farmer starts digging in one spot until the digging becomes difficult, then goes on to another spot. In the new spot he says 'its too crumbly here, I'll try another spot'. Next he hits a rock and for the rest of the day goes from spot to spot. The point here is that if the farmer had spent the same amount of time and energy in digging in one place he would soon go deep enough to find water. It is the same with choosing and reciting one's mantra. Persevere and stick with *one* mantra and one will find *living* water.

The continuous recitation of the mantra

The stages of the inner journey of meditation are reflected in the deepening of the mantra and the lessening effort to say it. At first we *say* the mantra despite the constant distractions. At one point we might *sound* the mantra with less effort and often uninterrupted by distractions. At another point we might *listen* to the mantra with a wholeheartedness that takes us beyond the power of distraction altogether. These stages can come and go cyclically.

Of course the mantra is a discipline, not an end in itself. It is a way of poverty of spirit; it is not the Kingdom itself. There may come a time, and this is a gift, when the mantra will lead us into absolute silence. This is not an experience to be anticipated, imagined or sought after. When one becomes *aware* they are silent one should simply resume saying the mantra, because the silence has been lost. If one is conscious of the silence, then one is not fully silent; if we *think* we are silent then we must return to the mantra.

The teaching of this tradition is that you say the mantra until you can no longer say it. We do not *choose* when to stop saying it. This ties into the ancient wisdom of the desert fathers: 'the monk who knows he is praying, is not praying, the monk who does not know he is praying is praying'.

John Main, in reply to a question about the mantra leading us to silence, reminds us that we cannot make silence happen. He says:

> The gift of pure prayer, the gift of pure contemplation, the gift of pure silence is an absolute gift. It is never something that we can, as it were, earn or twist God's arm to get. When it is given, we accept it with joy and then we say our mantra again.

Saying the mantra at other times

The mantra can definitely be repeated outside of our daily periods of meditation. This tradition ties in directly with St Paul's admonition to 'Pray unceasingly' (1 Thess. 5:17).

Once the mantra is rooted through our daily practice over a period of years, we might begin to hear the mantra sounding within, without having to do all of the work ourselves. In the beginning we repeat the mantra at the surface level of the mind. But as we persevere, the mantra becomes more deeply rooted in our consciousness. Again for the Christian this rooting ties into St Paul's injunction to 'pray unceasingly'. Bishop Theophane the Recluse (1815–94) writes that after the initial effort of saying our prayer word the prayer becomes like a brook that murmurs in the heart.

And this of course is when the mantra is a great source of consolation and strength in times of crisis, trauma and even pain. Meditators constantly talk about the power of the mantra to divert our attention and therefore offer relief from pain and anxiety. But beyond this, when we say our mantra we are calling upon God at

THE MANTRA/PRAYER WORD AND ITS ROLE 47

the deepest level of our being. This is where our faith and grace enters into meditation.

One meditator recently recounted an incident after surgery. As he woke up after the anaesthesia wore off he was welcomed by the mantra sounding loud and clear within with no effort to say it required on his part. More importantly he felt it was like an old friend welcoming him back to the land of the living and offering him support and encouragement for the approaching convalescent period.

The mantra releases a deep inner spiritual strength. And as mentioned, sometimes the mantra will spontaneously arise in our consciousness in our daily routine. This is a great blessing and again a gift of God. Father John once said 'first say the Mantra at the time of meditation, and then (soon) it will begin to sound within at other times of the day'.

The poverty of the mantra

John Cassian speaks of the purpose of meditation as that of restricting the mind to the poverty of the single verse. A little later, he shows his full meaning in an illuminating phrase. He talks about becoming 'grandly poor'. Meditation will certainly give you new insights into poverty. As you persevere with the mantra, you will begin to understand more and more deeply, out of your own experience, what Jesus meant when He said, 'Blessed are the poor in spirit'. . . . In meditation, then, we declare our own poverty. We renounce words, thoughts, imagination and we do so by restricting the mind to the poverty of one word.

(JOHN MAIN, *Word Into Silence*)

As John Main points out, it was the desert monk John Cassian who talked clearly about the poverty of repeating a formula (mantra) in unceasing prayer (see Chapter 8). In his Tenth Conference Cassian says:

This the formula which the mind should unceasingly cling to until, strengthened by the constant use of it and by continual meditation, it casts off and rejects the rich and ample matter of all manner of thoughts and restricts itself to the poverty of a single verse.

Cassian related the poverty of reciting a single verse in prayer to the beatitude 'blessed are the poor in spirit for theirs is the kingdom of heaven'.

John Main felt that the real poverty in meditation is, as John Cassian says, restricting the activity of our mind to the poverty of a single verse. Father John also pointed out that meditation as a way of poverty is also experienced in the words of Jesus: 'the person who finds his life must lose it' (Matt. 16:25). We enter into a way of prayer says Father John, that demands total poverty, total renunciation, total faith and a total 'letting go'. Of course this 'letting go' is not easy. St Augustine once prayed 'Dear God make me chaste . . . but not yet'.

Of course there is another ascesis that develops through meditation and that is a detachment not so much from material possessions as from *covetousness*. This was the core of the message of Jesus 'How happy are the poor'. It is only when we have stopped clinging not only to words, thoughts and images but also to other attachments that we truly find liberation on the path of meditation.

And we must never forget Jesus was poor. He was born in a stable, had nowhere to lay his head during his public life and died in absolute poverty. As long as we *covet* material possessions and other attachments and cling to them we cannot be free. Meditation teaches us to let go of the chains of covetousness that keep us in bondage. That is why the words of Jesus mean so much to us: 'How happy are the poor'.

11
The mantra, distractions and the monkey mind

I want now to address a particular question that we all encounter. It is the question of distractions. What should you do when you begin to meditate and distracting thoughts come into your mind? The advice that the tradition has to give us is to ignore the distractions and to say your word and to keep on saying your word. Don't waste any energy in trying to furrow your brow and say, 'I will not think of what I'm going to have for dinner', or 'who I'm going to see today', or 'where am I going tomorrow', or whatever the distraction may be. Don't try to use any energy to dispel the distraction. Simply ignore it and the way to ignore it is to say your word.

(JOHN MAIN, *Moment of Christ*)

The role of the mantra in dealing with distractions

The problem all of us have in coming to an inner silence in meditation is that our minds are full of thoughts, images, sensations, emotions, insights, hopes, regrets, a never ending array of distractions.

St Teresa of Avila once said the human mind is like a boat where mutinous sailors have tied up the captain. The sailors all take a turn at steering the boat and of course the boat goes around in circles and eventually crashes on the rocks. That is our mind, says Teresa, full of thoughts taking us off in every direction. She also says 'Distractions and the wandering mind are part of the human condition and can no more be avoided than eating and sleeping'.

An Indian sage, Sri Ramakrishna, once said the human mind is like a great tree with monkeys jumping from branch to branch chattering away. Laurence Freeman in commenting on this story says there is a path that leads through this forest of chattering monkeys and it is the practice of reciting a mantra in our daily periods of meditation.

There is another wonderful story which illustrates the capricious human mind. In India the mind is often compared to the trunk of an elephant, restless, inquisitive and always straying.

In India if you watch an elephant in a parade you will see how apt the comparison is. In Indian towns and villages, elephants are often taken in religious processions through the streets to the temple. The streets are crooked and narrow, lined on either side with fruit stalls and vegetable stalls. Along comes the elephant with his restless trunk, and in one quick motion it grabs a whole bunch of bananas.

Eknath Easwaran, a teacher of meditation, says,

> you can almost see him asking, 'What else do you expect me to do? Here is my trunk and there are the bananas.' He just doesn't know what else to do with his trunk. He doesn't pause to peel the bananas, either, or to observe all the other niceties that masters of etiquette say should be observed in eating a banana. He takes the whole bunch, opens his wide mouth, and tosses the bananas in stalk and all. Then from the next stall he picks up a coconut and tosses it in after the bananas. There is a loud crack and the elephant moves on to the next stall. No threat can make this restless trunk settle down.
>
> But the wise trainer, if he knows his elephant well, will simply give that trunk a short bamboo stick to hold on to before the procession starts. Then the elephant will walk along proudly with his head up high, holding the bamboo stick in front of him like a drum major with a baton. He is not interested in bananas or coconuts any more, his trunk has something to hold on to.

The human mind is very much like this trunk of an elephant. Most of the time it has nothing to hold on to. But it can be kept from straying into the world of thoughts, imagination and fantasy by simply giving it something to hold on to – a mantra.

The mantra is a help towards concentration, enabling us to go beyond distractions, including words, thoughts, even holy thoughts. We say the mantra slowly, steadily with attentiveness. When we find our mind has wandered we simply come back to our mantra. We cannot force this way of prayer through sheer will power. Do not try too hard. Let go, relax. There is no need to fight or struggle with distractions. Simply return to the repetition of the mantra.

John Main also reminds us that we cannot attempt to force the elimination of distractions. In fact we must let go of goals and trying to achieve anything. The mantra will become rooted in our consciousness through the simple fidelity of returning to the mantra each morning and each evening. Meditation is centering ourselves on our inner core and allowing God to pray within us.

But a word of caution. The repetition of a mantra does not bring instant peace, harmony, the absence of distractions or silence. We must accept where we are on the pilgrimage of meditation. We should not get upset at continual distractions. Our aim is not to be free of *all* thoughts. Again this would be a goal and we do not want to have goals. John Main constantly advises us not to come to meditation with *any* expectations. So do not struggle and fret over distractions. The mantra simply expresses our *openness* to God and his indwelling presence.

Simone Weil, the French author, who died in 1943 at the age of 33, was an apostle of the spiritual life and defined prayer as *attention*. The mantra leads us to this attention. Another French spiritual writer, Pascal, felt the greatest enemy of prayer was the 'Gethsemani sleep' – when the apostles slept instead of watching with Jesus. Pascal felt that inattention and drowsiness were the enemies of prayer. Again the mantra helps us with this problem by bringing us to attention.

Do not get mad at distractions. This is a non-violent way of prayer. Ignore distractions by continually returning to the mantra. If one is distracted with thoughts 50 times in a period of meditation, when one returns to the mantra that is 50 times we have chosen God over the distractions.

A problem often observed by those meditating is that the thinking process continues even while saying the mantra. There is even a term for this. It is called *double tracking*. Again this is nothing to be concerned about. With perseverance the mantra will become stronger and our thoughts will diminish as the pilgrimage of meditation continues.

It is important to remember that when we are bombarded with thoughts and images at our time of meditation our will is still tuned in to the presence of God. To handle distractions we do require gentleness and patience. We have to wait, like the wise virgins, in patience and hope. Gentleness and patience indicate the Spirit is working silently within us. While we are aware of distractions we should never let them disturb us. We can even see the good in distractions; they keep us awake and on the journey. They come in one door and leave by another.

Despite all our efforts thoughts will come. Good thoughts, bad thoughts, 'urgent' reminders. Ignore them all. We just keep saying our word silently. We try to let go of thinking. We try to keep saying our word. We repeat the mantra silently and continuously in our hearts. The mantra will lead us to discipline, to concentration, to silence, to God.

Why saying the mantra is often so difficult: the light at the end of the tunnel

Some of the great saints, teachers and philosophers point out that coming to a state of stillness is a great challenge, even at times a quiet martyrdom. Lao Tzu (570–490 BC), the great Chinese philosopher, once described the handling of distractions:

> I do my utmost to attain emptiness;
> I hold firmly to stillness.
> The myriad creatures all rise together
> And I watch their return
> The teeming creatures
> All return to their separate roots.
> Returning to one's roots is known as stillness.

St Gregory of Sinai (fourteenth century) speaks of the effort and labour in this way of prayer and that one will be tempted to give up because of the continual pain in saying the mantra. But he says 'persevere persistently and with ardent longing seek the Lord in your heart'. *The Cloud of Unknowing* says 'this way of prayer is hard work, very hard work indeed . . . but on no account think of giving up'. A desert hermit, Abba Agatho said 'there is no labour as great as praying to God. Prayer is a mighty conflict to one's last breath.' So much for the challenge of the discipline of meditation!

There is, however, a great paradox here. It is true that the apophatic way of prayer is often one of darkness, a way of unknowing, and that God sometimes seems to have disappeared and we can no longer sense his presence. But at the same time this is often coupled with joy, inner peace and a firm conviction that we will find God in our aridity and distractedness through faith in his presence. At the same time as we are frustrated we nevertheless feel a mysterious yet powerful attraction to the indwelling Christ. And from time to time God will reveal his presence to us in the darkness. This is the work of grace.

John Main pin-points a good reason why the practice of meditation seems at times so difficult for us. He reminds us that Jesus says 'He who finds his life will lose it, and he who loses his life for my sake will find it' (Matt. 10:39). But as Father John points out we often become spiritual materialists, seeking to accumulate grace, virtue and merit. We are taught that success and winning is important in life, not losing. But meditation is a call to abandonment of all desire, a dispossession, a surrender and in a real sense it is losing one's life to God.

THE MANTRA, DISTRACTIONS AND THE MONKEY MIND 53

The key here is not to become over-anxious about what is 'happening' on the journey. Meditation requires a leap of trust into the unknown. God has a plan for each one of us and a particular path to follow. He already has the path mapped out. We have to be content *not* to see the way ahead. We have to let go of controlling, of knowing where we are on the journey. This is part of the death of the ego. Nikos Kazantzakis describes this letting go: 'God is fire and you must walk on it . . . dance on it. At that moment the fire will become cool water. But until you reach that point, what a struggle, my Lord, what agony!'

The habitual experience of dryness and endless distractions reminds us that the path of meditation is one of pure faith. In the Christian perspective this darkness and suffering will lead to light and life. The prophet Isaiah has given us encouragement when he says:

> Whoever walks in darkness
> And has no light shining for him
> let him trust in the name of Yahweh
> let him lean on his God (Isa. 50:10).

St Paul also reassures us 'you can trust God not to let you be tried beyond your strength, and with any trial he will give you a way out of it and the strength to bear it' (1 Cor. 10:13).

God is as present in darkness as in light. He is just as near in times of desolation as in times of consolation. Every spiritual journey has difficulties and setbacks, but the struggle to overcome them and to persevere is infinitely worthwhile. Trials and crosses can be baffling but are God's way of eliciting from us trust, abandonment and detachment on the spiritual journey. When we cry out in our weakness we have the consoling words of Jesus to St Paul 'My grace is sufficient for you, for my power is made perfect in weakness' (2 Cor. 12:9).

John Main does though give us hope when he points out that the recitation of our mantra should become easier as we persevere on the journey. With time the torrent of thoughts lessens and one enjoys a greater sense of calmness, stillness and inner peace. This transition is aptly depicted in the Russian spiritual classic *The Way of the Pilgrim*. At one point the Pilgrim is 'saying' the mantra, but one day he suddenly discovers the prayer 'says itself' and he hears it spontaneously arising and sounding within himself.

But again this 'sounding within' may only come after a lifetime of commitment to the meditative pilgrimage. Silence is a free gift of God and is not *earned*, or the mechanical outcome of reciting our mantra. What is important here is our *desire* for God, our *generosity*, our *openness* to his presence and above all our *faith*. We leave everything else in the hands of the Lord.

12
The body in meditation

The simple rule to remember is this – find a quiet place in your home or wherever you are at the time. Sit down and sit upright. Don't bother when you begin with too much of technique ... Sit upright. The essential rule of posture is that your spine is as upright as possible. Breathing – the simple rule is breathe. Do not get too het up about whether you should breathe in or breathe out. Do both! Then, the rule that is the most important of all – say your mantra, say your word. And that is the art of meditation, to learn to say it from the beginning to the end.

(JOHN MAIN, *Moment of Christ*)

As the psalmist says even the body longs for prayer: 'My heart and my flesh cry out for the living God' (Ps. 84). Because we are a single entity, body, mind and spirit, the body is a companion in meditation with the mind and spirit. For that reason we must respect, take care of and love the body and recognise this union and integration of body and spirit. St Paul was well aware of this and in the first letter to Corinthians says 'the body is for the Lord, and the Lord for the body' (1 Cor. 6:13).

In meditation we aim at a harmony of body and spirit. This is where the correct posture of an upright back plays an important role. Correct posture can assist us to remain alert and concentrated in our daily periods of meditation. If the body is steady, alert and still it strengthens and supports the spirit. We should sit comfortably with a straight back but not stiff or tense.

Certainly we do not want the body to be in discomfort or pain in meditation. This in itself will be a distraction and will interfere with our concentration in saying the mantra. Having said this it is obvious that one can still meditate when one is sick or even in pain. Whether it is healthy or sick, at ease or in pain, the role of the body is in the service of the Lord. St Paul speaking to the Romans said 'I beseech you therefore, by the mercies of God to offer your bodies as a living sacrifice, holy, acceptable to God which is your spiritual worship' (Rom. 12:1).

In meditation we try to keep the body as still as possible while keeping the back in an upright position. A still body has an effect on stilling the mind, while correct sitting posture will promote alertness, balance and harmony of spirit. Stillness helps us to realise that our bodies are sacred, 'temples of the Holy Spirit' (1 Cor. 6:19). And the Psalmist says: 'He leads me to the still waters; He restores my soul' (Psalm 23:2).

Correct breathing is also an important aspect of meditation. It is a good idea to take some deep breaths before meditating and to become aware for a few moments of one's breathing. Most people synchronise the saying of the mantra with their inhaling and exhaling. (See section to follow on breathing.)

No one can doubt the importance of body consciousness in prayer. Witness Christian monks chanting the Divine Office, Indians praying on the banks of the Ganges at dawn, Moslems prostrate before God at their daily times of prayer, Jews at the wailing wall or Zen Buddhist monks 'sitting'. St Paul saw this importance when he said to the Corinthians 'Glorify God in your body' (1 Cor. 6:20).

The relationship between yoga and meditation

The 5,000-year-old Hindu teaching on yoga, particularly the Hatha Yoga *asanas* and *pranayama* breathing can often be of great help in preparing the mind/body in meditation for quiet and silence. The late Benedictine monk Bede Griffiths felt strongly that in Christianity there is a tendency to deprecate the body and the senses and to elevate the intellect and the will as the unique sources of spiritual transformation. However as Father Bede points out there is an urgent need to recognise the place of matter and the body in the process of spiritual growth. The great yoga teachers of the past have always pointed out that the spiritual journey cannot be made without the body, which is God's gift to us at birth and is with us until death.

The origins of yoga are shrouded in the mists of time, but yoga is mentioned in the Indian scriptures, the Vedas, about 2500 BC, and was probably practised at an earlier date. The ancient Yogis had a profound understanding that on the spiritual path there must be an integrated development of body, mind and spirit and that these three must be in balance.

It is important to note, however, that yoga practice is not essential for those on the meditative path and in fact is not recommended for everyone, even by the Indian Yoga sages. Yoga is simply an aid, for those who choose it, to prepare the body for the discipline of meditation.

In a 36-minute video, Mary Stewart and Giovanni Felicioni show

how proper yoga breathing and sitting positions enable a more gentle integration of body, mind and spirit in meditation. This video is entitled 'The Body in Meditation: Yoga Exercises for the Christian Meditator'. This video features Hatha Yoga *asanas* or exercises as an aid in preparation for meditation. This video is available from the World Community for Christian Meditation, 23 Kensington Sq., London, W8 5HN, and outlets in various countries.

Posture in prayer

Blaise Pascal, the seventeenth-century French Christian apologist, once said 'all the troubles of life come upon us because we refuse to sit quietly for a while each day in our rooms'. A Zen Buddhist meditation saying reads 'sitting ... sitting and the grass grows greener'. There is also the story of St Sarapion, the Sidonite, a desert father of fourth-century Egypt. He travelled once on a pilgrimage to Rome. Here he was told of a celebrated recluse, a woman who lived always in one small room, never going out. Sceptical about her way of life, for he was himself a great wanderer, Sarapion called on her and asked: 'Why are you sitting here?' To this she replied: 'I am not sitting. I am on a journey.'

However, for those who associate prayer with their early childhood training of saying their prayers on their knees, sitting in meditation may at first seem strange. Yet this is an ancient practice in most of the world's religions. For 5,000 years Hindus have been meditating in the Lotus (sitting position). Zen Buddhists in particular are noted for their 'sitting' in meditation. In Christianity the early fourth-century desert monks sat weaving baskets or sewing while reciting a biblical mantra. Perhaps Richard Rolle, the fourteenth-century English hermit and contemplative has put it most succinctly for Christians:

> Sitting I am most at rest
> and my heart moves upward
> I have loved to sit, for
> thus I have loved God more
> and I remained
> longer within the comfort
> of love than if I were
> walking or standing or kneeling.

Sitting in an upright position in meditation allows us to breathe freely in saying our mantra. Sitting expresses receptiveness, self-surrender and particularly 'resting in God'. Sitting is an ideal posture for meditation because it roots us in attentiveness while at the same time allowing us to be relaxed. St Teresa of Avila once said 'we need no wings to go in search of God, but have only to find a place where we can *sit* alone and look upon God present within us'. That is a good definition of Christian Meditation but note the importance she gives to *sitting*.

Also a still body in sitting will have an effect on stilling the mind. However, we must be careful here. Too rigid an approach where we sit in fearful apprehension of moving can also be a distraction. A balance is required where we simply do our best in a given meditation period to sit in bodily stillness. The best plan is to sit in a position that will be comfortable so as to allow us to sit as still as possible during meditation. To sustain this sitting position we need to sit up straight, with back and neck in line but not rigid or tense.

In choosing a chair your feet should be flat on the floor. If a chair is too high place a cushion or book under your feet. The feet should be parallel with heels on the floor. A straight backed chair will be the best choice, but its comfort often depends on height or slope. A chair with arms will help prevent slumping. Look for a chair where one can sit alert but at the same time at ease. If possible it is best not to let the spine collapse against the back of the chair.

Prayer stools or prayer benches are quite popular today because one's legs and back are positioned comfortably in another symbolically prayerful position.

An alternative way of sitting on the floor involves a firm cushion and sitting on its forward edge. The head should remain in line with the trunk provided the cushion is not too high and pitches one forward. Legs should not be held out straight but folded. Pain and numbness can be a distraction here until flexibility is acquired in this position. The chin should not be thrust forward but tucked gently in. Shoulders should be relaxed and not slumped. The hands rest on the knees or lap.

Breathing and meditation

As mentioned, John Main with his Irish wit once said 'the only important thing about breathing is to continue to do so for the full time of your meditation'. But far from denigrating the role of breathing, John Main was well aware of its importance, especially in the practice of integrating the breath with the saying of the mantra. Only if it includes the body can Christian Meditation be truly a prayer of the whole person.

Because of the important balance between body, mind and spirit in meditation, correct breathing is recommended as one begins the daily practice. There is a Hindu saying: 'When the breath wanders the mind is unsteady, but when the breath is still, so is the mind still.' Physical breath is a scriptural symbol of God's spirit.

However, the problem for so many people who come to meditate is that they breathe poorly so that their lungs are never fully used; only a small proportion of the seventy million alveoli in our lungs are extended. There is a tendency for some people who meditate to breathe shallowly through the mouth and make little use of the diaphragm (abdomen) when they inhale. This results in only the top part of the lungs being used with only a small amount of oxygen inhaled. Tension usually results from rapid shallow breathing from the top of our lungs. Our aim in meditation is to slowly breathe deeply from our abdomen. St Paul would understand the process in the light of his advice to the Romans 'make every part of your body into a weapon fighting on the side of God' (Rom. 6:13).

Breathing in meditation should be a slow, natural rhythmic action involving the entire torso. Ideally breathing correctly means breathing through the nose with the mouth closed and the lungs fully inhaling and exhaling. Breathing out should normally take twice as long as the in-breath. The more stale air we can exhale the more fresh air we can inhale. The breath itself should be calm and deep. Deep breathing will calm the nervous system.

Integrating the saying of the mantra with the inhaling/exhaling process seems to come naturally and spontaneously to almost everyone who meditates. Often no conscious effort is required. Perhaps this is why John Main was hesitant to place emphasis on any particular breathing practice. He recognised that without any conscious effort on their part most meditators adapt the mantra spontaneously to their breathing.

However, for those newcomers who wish to have some idea of how to adapt the mantra to their breathing, here are a few examples of how this can be done with the mantra ma-ra-na-tha. Please bear in mind that the choice of these examples will vary for different individuals, depending on their lung capacity. There is no *right* way to do it. One could for instance say the entire mantra breathing in, while breathing out in silence. Or one could say ma-ra breathing in and na-tha breathing out. There are also other combinations, again, usually depending on one's lung capacity.

What is most important is to come to a comfortable rhythmic pattern reciting the mantra in conjunction with one's breathing and build this discipline into one's meditative practice. Again for many people no conscious effort will be required to accomplish this.

The physiological benefits of meditation

If your teeth are not up to par you might take heart from a recent headline in a North American paper, 'Meditating 40 minutes a day can help battle tooth decay'. The article went on to say studies have shown meditators have saliva that is lower in acid and bacteria and hence resists decay to tooth enamel.

Or how about this? The *USA Today* newspaper recently quoted Dr Herbert Benson, author of several books on meditation, as saying '34% of his infertile patients get pregnant within six months, 78% of insomniacs become regular sleepers and doctor's visits for pain are reduced 36%, all through regular periods of meditation'. It is all very interesting, but take it all with a pinch of spiritual salt.

On a more serious note we do know scientists have done innumerable clinical studies on meditators which indicate a lower oxygen consumption during meditation, decrease in serum lactate levels (relaxation), reductions in systolic and diastolic blood pressure, lower heartbeat, a relaxation of muscle tension and a boost to the immune system.

Since we are one entity, body, mind and spirit, these bodily side effects of meditating can be accepted graciously with thanks. However, what is important to keep in mind here is that any physiological benefits of meditation are quite secondary, or one might say *signs* rather than the essential meaning of meditation.

In his 200 taped Christian Meditation talks, John Main rarely mentions any of the physiological benefits of meditation. Father John obviously felt that lower blood pressure or reduced oxygen consumption paled into insignificance when one considers meditation is a spiritual path into the presence of the indwelling Christ. In other words Father John felt we must keep our priorities straight. Meditation is primarily a faith-filled spiritual discipline and any side effects helpful to the body should be considered quite secondary.

However, meditators are often aware of greater physical vitality and energy, which has led to the aphorism that 'meditators have 25 hour days'. In other words the one hour we devote to meditation is not lost time for we seem to get the investment of time back with interest even in the physiological sphere.

13
The practice of Christian Meditation

The central message of the New Testament is that there is really only one prayer and that is the prayer of Christ. It is a prayer that continues in our hearts day and night. It is the stream of love that flows constantly between Jesus and his Father. It is the Holy Spirit.

It is the most important task of any fully human life to become as open as possible to this stream of love. We have to allow this prayer to become our prayer, to enter into the experience of being swept beyond ourselves into this wonderful prayer of Jesus – this great cosmic river of love.

In order for us to do this we must learn a most demanding discipline that is a way of silence and stillness. It is as though we have to create a space within ourselves that will allow the consciousness of the prayer of Jesus to envelop us in this powerful mystery.

(JOHN MAIN, *Moment of Christ*)

The time and place for meditation

Morning and evening are traditional times of prayer in most of the world's religions including Christianity. The monastic tradition in Christianity starts the day with Lauds (morning prayer) and ends the day with Compline (night prayer).

In the morning nature is usually calm and quiet and most people feel the best time to meditate is immediately after getting up and before breakfast and the day's activities. John Main felt it was always advantageous to meditate before rather than after a meal. In the morning we place God first in our priorities. Before the outer world calls there is a call to enter the inner world of stillness.

The evening period of meditation usually presents a greater challenge for most people. Because we all lead such different lives it is difficult to lay down any general guidelines for the evening time of meditation. Again, if possible, it would be desirable to meditate before the evening meal and before the digestive process begins.

However this is not always possible and many people choose a later hour in the evening. Some people are 'night people' and are wide awake and concentrated in the late evening. For others a late evening meditation would simply result in sleepiness and 'nodding off'.

Sometimes choosing a time for meditation requires ingenuity. A mother of nine children who meditates finds a magic half-hour in mid-afternoon when some of her children are sleeping and other children have not yet arrived home from school. Because of the busyness and activities of the day and perhaps tiredness, it might be a good idea to take a shower before the evening meditation or at the very least splash water on one's face. Regularity and punctuality are important aspects of morning and evening meditation. It is advantageous to try and build a regular rhythm and pattern of set times to meditate each day.

In regard to location it is recommended (if possible) to meditate in the same location each day. The goal here would be to meditate in a definite place set aside for stillness; a place simply to *be*. One person will use the basement, or perhaps a portion of a kitchen overlooking trees and flowers; another meditator has cleared out a small room and equipped it with a prayer bench, small table with candle and a Bible. If the opportunity is available, some people like to meditate outdoors in gardens, parks, on river banks and other locations where they feel close to nature.

Thomas Merton once advised, 'there should be at least a room or some corner where no one will find you and disturb you and notice you. You should be able to untether yourself from the world and set yourself free, loosing all the fine strings and strands of tension that bind you, by sight, by sound, by thought.'

Certainly our surroundings can be an assist in coming to stillness. And often our prayer room will be a sign to other family members that we are not to be disturbed in our time of meditation. Not only do we have to give priority to those daily times of meditation, but also a priority to our spiritual environment.

Children and meditation

Some children seem to take to meditation like a duck takes to water. Not only *can* children meditate but they *need* meditation in their daily lives. Children today have stress, tension, competitiveness, noise, often excessive activity and over-stimulation. They do need to balance their lives with inner stillness. And the interesting observation of parents and teachers is that once given the encouragement to meditate children come to love their daily quiet times.

They enjoy a place to just 'be'. Moreover they seem to have less self-consciousness than adults and with their unquestioning faith are readily able to bring their external senses to inner calmness. Many children meditate with their parents. Children are often influenced by simply *seeing* their parents meditating and witnessing the fruits of their parents' daily practice. This influence of parents who meditate can be incalculable in its effects on children. Small children will often peek into the meditation room to see what their parents are up to. They will soon connect a mother and father who are more patient, cheerful and kind, with their parents' daily practice of meditation.

As for the length of time for children to meditate, the rule of thumb is for children to meditate for one minute of each year of their lives. A children's Christian Meditation group in Dublin meditates for 14 minutes at the weekly meeting of twenty 13, 14 and 15-year-old boys and girls. Their leader gives them a choice of a number of mantras.

It has been said however that the best time to start a child on the path of meditation is when the child is in the womb. We now know the fetus is alert and sensitive to its mother's emotional vibrations whether it is anger, stress, calmness or stillness. A meditating mother passes her calming inner stillness in an intuitive way to her child. The benefits of introducing young children to meditate will become even more obvious in early adult years.

One way to introduce children to stillness in meditation is through the dramatisation of biblical stories. For example the parent or teacher could recount the story by three of the evangelists about Jesus asleep in the boat. A great storm arises, with a fierce wind and gigantic waves. The apostles are terrified, afraid the boat is going to swamp. They cry out to Jesus to save them. Jesus wakes and says 'Why are you frightened' (Matt. 8:26). He says to the wind and waves 'be calm'. At this point the parent/teacher can say 'now let us spend a few moments being calm and still, letting God be with us'. Of course it is also important to explain to children that while Jesus was present in the biblical stories, he is equally present within us now in spirit.

For further thought about meditation and children see the book *Born Contemplative* by Sister Madeleine Simon.

Meditation and self-hypnosis

A question often asked is, whether Christian Meditation is a form of self-hypnosis. They are really quite the opposite. Self-hypnosis is a goal-directed experience through self-suggestion, aimed at changing one's feelings, thoughts and fantasies and general wellbeing. Self-hypnosis is involved with imagination and in self-guided imagery utilising the senses. It is a little like day-dreaming, using thoughts and imagination to define reality and change one's frame of mind. It is a very self-conscious, self-preoccupied exercise. A recent book on self-hypnosis says it can help stop smoking, lose weight, get rid of crippling fear, and ease headaches and asthma.

The practice of Christian Meditation, on the other hand, is not goal-directed but God-centred and is meant to lead us into the mystery that is beyond thoughts, imagination and feelings. It is a way of prayer that gradually leads us beyond self-consciousness. In meditation we come to experience the true meaning of the words of Jesus, 'Anyone who wishes to be a follower of mine must leave *self* behind' (Matt. 16:24).

Tests of brain waves during meditation show that they differ substantially from those that occur during sleep or any form of hypnosis.

Music and meditation

Listening to music with its calming effect can be an excellent way to prepare for our daily periods of silent meditation. Pythagoras (582–500 BC), the Greek philosopher, sang calming melodies to his followers with the firm conviction that melody and rhythm restore harmony to the human soul. According to his biographer, Pythagoras held that music 'contributes greatly' to one's health, in the evening easing the 'perturbations and tumults' of the day, and in the morning freeing one 'from nocturnal heaviness and torpor'. The first book of Samuel points out that King Saul's fits of depression were alleviated by the music of young David.

On the physiological level music has been proven to produce beneficial changes in heartbeat, breathing rhythm, blood pressure, pulse rate, hormone levels and immune response. Music perhaps more than any other form of art has the power to create immediate mood and atmosphere, and in elevating the spirit changes our consciousness beneficially.

Perhaps this is why many Christian Meditation group leaders and individual meditators like to start meditation and end meditation with the playing of suitable music. To assist meditators, the Christian Meditation Centre at 29 Campden Hill Rd., London W8 7DX, has produced for sale a number of pre-programmed tapes of choral, gregorian chant and light classical music. These tapes are also available in Canada at Box 376, Thessalon, Ontario, POR 1LO. The tapes consist of two and a half minutes of opening music, 25

THE PRACTICE OF CHRISTIAN MEDITATION

minutes of silence, followed by two and a half minutes of closing music. Those meditators with two cassette slots in their tape recorder often record their own tapes with their personal music preference. One additional advantage of this musical timing system is that one is no longer disturbed by loud PINGS from timers or no longer has to look at one's watch to determine the end of the meditation period.

The importance of the 'heart' in meditation

> *Speaking to*
> *the Little Prince*
> *about love and life,*
> *the Fox says:*
> *And now here*
> *is my secret,*
> *a very simple secret.*
> *It is only*
> *with the heart*
> *that one can see rightly;*
> *What is essential*
> *is invisible*
> *to the eye.*
> (ANTOINE DE SAINT-EXUPÉRY, 1900–1944, *The Little Prince*)

Meditation is often referred to as the 'prayer of the heart'. Perhaps the best definition of the heart is that it is the deep centre, the core of our being, the place of unity where body, mind and spirit are one. We often say we want to get to the *heart* of the matter. The heart is the *centre* of a person, the centre from which we relate to God and to others. St John of the Cross says God is the centre of my soul. If we do 'something from our heart' we do it with our deepest feelings, from our very centre.

Heart is also a rich biblical concept. Ezekiel says hardness of heart is a sin, and that we need 'contrite' hearts. St Paul prays that 'Christ may dwell in our hearts in love'. The *heart* in the Old Testament Semitic understanding of the word meant the deepest reaches of one's inner being where love is generated in self-sacrifice for the one loved.

The heart is known as our 'inner being'. The heart is the spiritual centre of our being where God lives. Scripture tells us the source of prayer is the heart. Heart also has to do with 'openness'. When we say 'have a heart' we mean be open to me, be kind, be receptive. When we are wholehearted we commit and give ourselves fully to someone or to a cause. When someone is stubborn or closed we say that person is hard-hearted or cold-hearted. When we deal with a warm-hearted person we know we will be treated kindly, our sorrows and joys will be shared. It is in our heart that we are aware of ourselves and of God. Perhaps that is the deepest meaning of heart. In meditation we say God touches our heart or we seek God in the silence and stillness of our own heart. When we give someone our heart we give ourselves completely. That is why we often call meditation the prayer of the heart, because we give ourselves completely to Christ in the deepest part of our spiritual being – our heart. Meditation is the place where we encounter God in the depths of our own heart.

The heart has also been defined as 'the deepest psychological ground of one's personality' and 'the root and source of all one's own inner truth'.

It was the desert fathers who introduced the term 'prayer of the heart' which meant a total surrender to God when one had abandoned mental images of God and brought 'the mind into the heart'. This Hesychast tradition of the desert monks was defined as a 'straining toward God' but with a deep understanding that ultimately prayer is the operation of the indwelling Trinity praying within us. These early monks saw the heart as a 'still point' where God and man meet in silent self-surrender and self-giving.

Taking off one's shoes while meditating

There is an ancient tradition for taking one's shoes off during meditation. In the Old Testament Moses meets God in the burning bush. The first thing God says is 'take off your sandals in the presence of the Lord' (Exod. 3:5). Some meditators like to follow this pattern of taking off their shoes 'in the presence of the Lord' during their meditation periods. However it is always an optional choice. For some people this tradition would simply be a distraction.

Again some meditators treat their meditation room as a shrine, a holy place, and it seems to make sense to them to take off their shoes which may carry in the contamination of the streets. On a practical level taking off one's shoes can simply be more comfortable. However each meditator should feel free to make their own choice in this matter.

Meditating more than twice a day

The traditional teaching, especially for newcomers, is to give priority to building a morning and evening meditation into the pattern of one's life. For busy people with family and community responsibilities this is all that is required. One has to start gently and simply commit oneself to this twice-daily spiritual discipline. After some time of meditating regularly and faithfully, and if the circumstances of one's life permit, by all means put in a midday period of meditation if you wish. When a discipline is established here the schedule becomes more natural. The Spirit will be the teacher here. However, John Main does point out that we must be careful not to take a materialistic approach to meditation; if two times are good why not three, if three times are good, why not four, etc. etc. *More* meditation periods do not necessarily mean *better*.

Falling asleep during meditation

In meditation we are trying to do two very opposite things, be alert and yet at the same time be relaxed. When we doze off the relaxation aspect of meditation has taken over from our alertness and concentration. Usually this happens when we are beginning the path of meditation. As we persevere in the discipline and grow in attention to the saying of the mantra, and listening to the *sound* of the mantra, wakefulness deepens with the silence and there is less of a tendency to doze off.

Falling asleep can be caused by meditating late in the evening when we are extremely tired. However some meditators are 'night people' and are very alert and wide awake late in the evening. Meditation after consuming alcohol or after a heavy meal can also lead to a lack of wakeful attention to the mantra and dozing off. Drowsiness can also have much to do with our posture and our breathing in meditation. (See Chapter 12 on the body in meditation.)

As previously mentioned, to counteract sleepiness or tiredness try splashing cold water on your face before meditation or even consider taking a bath or shower. At times though it will be necessary to dispel drowsiness and make a real effort at being alert. So when you feel a 'doze' coming on check your posture and breathing and make a conscious effort to deal with the problem.

However you must not feel guilty about falling asleep. God loves us asleep or awake. Our role is simply to make the effort to stay awake; a reminder of the words of Jesus to his disciples 'Could you not watch one hour with me?' (Mark 14:37).

Psychic phenomena, visions and voices

John Main along with the great teachers of meditation down the ages felt that, faced with any kind of psychic phenomena such as visions, voices, celestial odours, clairvoyance, levitation, the person meditating should treat them as distractions and gently return to saying the mantra. He once said: 'we don't come to meditation to experience the experience'.

In reference to these experiences, St John of the Cross suggested we resist and run away from all such phenomena:

> And it must be known that although all these things may happen to the bodily senses in the way of God, we must never rely upon them or accept them, but must fly from them, without trying to ascertain whether they be good or evil; for, the more completely exterior and corporeal they are, the less certainly they are of God . . . So he that esteems such things errs greatly and exposes himself to great peril of being deceived; in any case he will have within himself a complete impediment to the attainment of spirituality.
>
> (*Collected Works of John of the Cross*)

Self-deception is more than a possibility with these kinds of experiences as well as spiritual pride. Our ego could even develop an attachment to any of these parapsychological phenomena and that would be a great hindrance to our spiritual growth. The general rule is to ignore such phenomena. Christian Meditation is a path of pure faith, a way of unknowing and often a way of darkness. Psychic phenomena are simply distractions during our times of meditation.

There are of course spiritual gifts and graces that come to us at certain times in our spiritual journey. At times they might serve as encouragement and consolation, at times *touches* calling us to seek God more fervently. How does one determine what comes from God and what is hallucination, what is reality and what is unreality? If there is any confusion here a spiritual guide may be of some help in discerning their real source (see Chapter 20 on Spiritual Guides). Advice might also be sought within one's Christian Meditation group.

A good rule of thumb is to be cautious in not attributing every kind of experience to the Holy Spirit. And never seek such *experiences* in Meditation. We should come to the journey of meditation with no goals and no expectations. Authentic contemplative prayer is never measured by 'spiritual experiences' but by the seeking of God's will and surrender to his love.

THE PRACTICE OF CHRISTIAN MEDITATION

On missing one's daily meditation period

A question arises whether one should feel guilty about missing a period of meditation. The only thing to feel guilty about is feeling guilty! There is enough religious guilt amongst Christians without adding to the burden of guilt.

Fidelity to the morning and evening meditation is important but there will be times when through the circumstances of our life or our own lack of discipline we miss a period of meditation. It takes time to establish discipline and discipline is a way of liberty not restriction. Meditators often point out they feel a gap in their day when this happens. But please, whether it is deliberate or not, do not feel guilty. Simply come back the next day with renewed commitment to the path. What is important is to hang in there for the long run. And a false sense of guilt has no part to play on the path of Christian Meditation. Jesus calls us to repentance, not guilt.

Interior silence is not a void

A number of questions arise regarding the mind in meditation. Do we try to make our minds blank or void in Christian Meditation? Can emptying the mind be dangerous? Will it make me vulnerable to undesirable forces and influences?

The interior silence we open ourselves to in meditation is filled with the presence of God. Sometimes it is not a *felt* presence, but the special knowledge we call faith means we can 'know' in our times of meditation that the indwelling Trinity actively lives and prays within us. Prayer is really not *doing* but *being*. It has nothing to do with making one's mind a void or our inner being becoming a vacuum.

The repetition of our mantra will keep us alert, concentrated and free from any kind of void or blankness. Meditation is based on faith, and this faith will keep us aware of God's presence.

Silence in meditation is a gift from God and all God asks is our self-surrender, our love and our desire to rest in him. At our still point we find not a void, but God who is love. However, the way to this is by leaving behind our ego and self-centredness of every kind. (See Chapter 20 on the 'ego'.)

The author of *The Cloud of Unknowing* (see Chapter 8) points out that Satan cannot enter this inner chamber of one's heart in this prayer. He says that in this silence one can only be open to the voice of the Spirit who dwells within us.

God's language is silence

It is said that God's language is *silence*. So God does not speak to us with a booming voice from heaven but like Elijah we will hear God speak to us in the silence.

On the path of meditation we will certainly come to know *how* God has 'spoken' to us. We will see the decisions made, the pitfalls avoided, the right path followed and we will know that God has spoken to us. But we will not hear the voice of God in our times of meditation in any ordinary sense of that term. In our meditation periods, God speaks *directly* to our heart. God's language indeed is *silence*.

Of course when it comes to hearing God speak to us there may be times when we will not be absolutely certain we have heard his voice and what the right thing to do is in certain instances. For this reason we need both faith, deep listening, and sometimes the wise counsel of others.

Sacred places to meditate

A question that is often raised is 'is it necessary to meditate in church or can we meditate anywhere?' Meister Eckhart says 'God is equally in all things and in all places'. It is true that the presence of Christ takes many forms. He is present in the Eucharist under the form of bread and wine, but he is also present in the worshipping community, the Scriptures, and is present in our hearts as well as at our times of meditation.

As Eckhart says when Christ is present, he is wholly present. He is not *more* present in the Blessed Sacrament and *less* present in the worshipping community or in our hearts during meditation. So for that reason the place where a person meditates is *holy ground*, whether it is a church, a bus, beside a river, in a prison, a garden or one's home.

John Main pointed out in *The Present Christ*, that God cannot be more or less present, as God is indivisible.

On insights during meditation

Sometimes people feel that if an inspiration or some reminder or creative idea comes during their meditation period they should write it down or at least try and remember it. However, meditation is a spiritual discipline and we try to ignore these kinds of distractions by simply returning to our mantra. The experience of most meditators is that if we go back to the mantra with faithfulness each time we get a creative idea, we will subsequently remember

THE PRACTICE OF CHRISTIAN MEDITATION

these creative thoughts at the end of our meditation. Once we desire to hang on to a great idea or inspiration we are caught up in self-consciousness and then concern about forgetting the idea. The best idea is to ignore all creative thought by going each time to the reciting of the mantra. Meditation is very much about 'letting go'.

The gift of tears

Once often hears of meditators who have begun to cry at different times, participating in the Eucharist, reading Scripture, at the time of spiritual reading and at other times. This is often called the 'gift of tears'.

The experience of weeping or having compunction for one's sins, known as *penthos*, or the gift of tears, is a gift from God. St Benedict, in between writing a rule for monks and founding Western monasticism, also wept it seems at the most unexpected times.

The gift of tears is a charism well known to the early desert fathers/mothers who saw it as a sign of a second baptism, not by water but by the Holy Spirit. St John Climacus comments on this: 'Greater than baptism itself is the fountain of tears after baptism.' This same saint added, 'tears shed from fear intercede for us; but tears of all-holy love show us that our prayer has been accepted.'

The gift of tears is a melt-down of our heart of stone being replaced by a heart of flesh. The prophet Ezekiel says:

> A new heart I will give you, and a new spirit I will put within you; I will take out of your flesh the heart of stone and give you a heart of flesh. And I will put my spirit within you ... and you shall be my people, and I will be your God. (Ezek. 36:26–28)

The gift of tears is a sign of an interior conversion, a metanoia and compunction at the core of our being.

However, like all charisms, it is a gift. One must also be aware there can be neurotic tears and tears that flow from hysteria. The sign of the true gift of tears is an abiding inner peace, joy and love deep in one's heart.

Neither male nor female

A question often raised is why more women than men seem to meditate. This seems to vary from country to country. In Australia Laurence Freeman once noticed that the majority of the 300-plus meditators in the room were men!

Dr Jack Dominian, a well known psychiatrist and marriage counsellor, points out that when women pray they pray from their heart more than their mind. Prayer for women, he says, 'really arises from the heart and is a connection with God as a *loving* person'. He believes this experience of God is made much more easily by women and that men take a more *rational* approach to faith and spirituality.

In a recent article in *The Tablet*, Annabel Miller talks about a discussion with Cardinal Basil Hume OSB in which the Cardinal describes the Jesus prayer. 'The art of that prayer', he said, 'is to repeat it slowly and go on. There is a sense in which he whom you are addressing seems to be present.' Ms Miller asked the Cardinal whether one could describe his experience of resting passively in the presence of God, rather than actively seeking him, as the working of his *feminine* side. 'Yes I think you could', he replied. 'It is Mary of Bethany sitting at the feet of Christ.'

With changing gender rolls today perhaps the challenge for active men is to learn to sit and wait before the Lord.

Another aspect of women's yearning for interiority is a greater understanding of Julian of Norwich's revelation that God 'is truly our mother'. Louis Dupré and James Wiseman in *Light from Light: an Anthology of Christian Mysticism* point out that Julian's attribution of motherhood to Jesus is very prominent in her writings. The authors state:

> In Julian the creative and redemptive words of 'Jesus our mother' are regularly brought together as when she writes that 'Jesus is our true mother in nature by our first creation and he is our true mother in grace by his taking our created nature. All the lovely words and all the sweet loving offices of beloved motherhood are appropriated to the second person . . .'

Recent scholarship has shown that the allusions to God's motherhood in Scripture had already been elaborated by some of the Fathers of the Church and that the motherhood of Jesus was a favourite subject of many Cistercian writers of the twelfth century.

In his book *Why Not be a Mystic*, Frank X. Tuoti points out that the Eastern churches traditionally ascribed the feminine principle to God the Holy Spirit with the term 'Hagia Sophia', Holy Wisdom. Says Tuoti 'Eastern orthodoxy has never had to deal with the false problem of whether God is masculine or feminine, understanding that God is both and neither, but is pure Spirit transcending gender and beyond all anthropomorphic interpretations.'

The late Benedictine monk Bede Griffiths has provided an insightful video on this subject entitled 'Discovering the Feminine' (More Than Illusion Films, Sydney, Australia).

Measuring the spiritual

Can we evaluate our spiritual progress in meditation? In the first place it is a truism that we cannot measure the spiritual. We can measure the depths of the oceans and the number of galaxies but we simply cannot measure the spiritual in any normal way. The only real test of spiritual growth is an increase in simplicity, compassion and love.

In addition, what happens in our daily times of meditation is not of great importance. Usually nothing happens. Meditation is not about entering into an altered state of consciousness or seeing and experiencing anything out of the ordinary. Wondering about our spiritual progress is really part of the self-centredness we are meant to leave behind in meditation.

Evelyn Underhill (1875–1941) who devoted her lifetime to the study of prayer and spirituality was adamantly against checking one's spiritual pulse and once said 'It is quite impossible for any of us to measure ourselves and estimate our progress'.

Meditation is in fact all about *not* looking for progress or results. As John Main says, it is about taking the searchlight off ourselves, it is about losing our self-consciousness. If we start asking questions about 'How far have I come?' or 'How long is all of this going to take me?' or 'Am I becoming holier?' then we are becoming self-conscious – something we want to avoid. Meditation, says Father John, requires simplicity and we are led to that simplicity by faithfully saying the mantra.

So we do not evaluate our progress in meditation. But experience shows that meditation will gradually transform our lives into love – if we persevere. Above all, we should not evaluate our progress in what happens during the actual times of meditation. Sometimes we will be silent, sometimes totally distracted. If we want to evaluate progress, look to the inner transformation into love and compassion for others which is taking place in our daily lives.

And yet in another way we can get some sense of our spiritual growth. It does not take a long time on the path of meditation before St Paul's fruits of prayer begin their work within us. St Paul's 'harvest of the Spirit' includes love, joy, peace, patience, kindness, goodness, fidelity, gentleness and self-control (Gal 5:22). All of these gifts are released to us as we learn to listen to the language of the heart which is silence. But these gifts extend outwards to others in our family, the community, our work situation and in all aspects of our daily life and relationships.

We can also judge our progress (if we must) by observing a growth of interest in Scripture, the sacramental life, love of neighbour, compassion for others and a developing sense of justice. (See Chapter 15 on the relationship between prayer and action.)

There is a beautiful story from the desert fathers which suggests how we might evaluate our spiritual growth.

> Abbot Lot came to Abbot Joseph and said: Father, according as I am able, I keep my little rule, and my little fast, my prayer, meditation and contemplative silence; and according as I am able I strive to cleanse my heart of thoughts: now what more should I do? The elder rose up in reply and stretched out his hands to heaven, and his fingers became like ten lamps of fire. He said: Why not be totally changed into fire?
>
> (THOMAS MERTON, *Wisdom of the Desert*)

That *is* the question about progress. Are we being gradually changed into the fire of love through meditation?

Finally a voice from the past, Gregory of Nyssa (335–95) reminds us that evaluating spiritual progress has much to do with undue expectations on the spiritual path. Gregory reminds us about the incomprehensibility of God and that the experience of God's presence will never fully satisfy us. All we can do is persevere in our life of prayer with hope, faith and love and leave everything in the hands of God.

14
Christian Meditation and other ways of prayer

Walter Hilton is a very good witness that there is no antipathy as it were between contemplative prayer, vocal prayer, liturgical prayer. He does trace a kind of progressive development through these forms but not in the sense that we ever get to a stage in our life when we have gone beyond liturgical prayer or vocal prayer. The development he really sees is a growth in the delight with which one enters into whatever form is appropriate at any time. And all these forms of prayer are, of course, complementary, provided that we know them as they really are: as entrances into the eternal prayer of Jesus which is his loving return to the Father. At all times in our lives all the various streams of prayer are coming together and binding us ever more closely to the Lord Jesus in the universal ocean of his prayer.

(JOHN MAIN, *Christian Meditation: The Gethsemani Talks*)

Praying and praying for . . .

It is important to understand the role of petitionary prayer in relation to the practice of meditation. We can see the role of petitionary prayer in the celebration of the Eucharist, not only in the intentions of the prayer of the faithful but in the Our Father itself which is a prayer of petition. Jesus himself says 'Whatever you ask for in my name will be given to you' (John 14:13). St Paul in the introduction of his epistles is always praying for others and constantly says 'I remember you in my prayers'.

In Luke 22:31–32, Jesus says 'Simon, Simon . . . I have prayed for you that your faith may not fail'. In the gospel of Matthew Jesus says: 'Ask and it will be given you; seek and you will find; knock and it will be opened to you' (7:7). Throughout the ages the Christian community has prayed for its special needs. This intercessary prayer therefore will always be an important part of our spiritual life.

However, perhaps at times we overdo the prayer of petition. At a retreat recently someone reacted against 'the prayer of silence' by saying she had 68 people with assorted aches and pains, a laundry list that she must bring before the Lord each day. She referred to this as 'getting my prayers in'. And yet Jesus makes it clear that babbling on in many words is counter-productive. In Matthew 6:7–8 he says: 'In your prayers do not babble as the pagans do, for they think that by using many words they will make themselves heard. Do not be like them. Your Father knows what you need before you ask Him.' God, all-knowing, all-seeing, knows our *real* needs much better than we know them ourselves. This means that all our petitions for ourselves and others can be brought silently before the Lord in an instant of recollection as we begin our times of silent meditation.

The problem with petitionary prayer is that we can become more attached to God's gifts than to God himself. We cannot twist God's arm into giving us things. The prayer of the faithful in the Eucharist is not so much to inform God what we need, because God already knows our real needs. Petitionary prayer is really for the good of those who hear the petitions. We are not so much addressing God, as sharing our needs and concerns with the eucharistic community in the faith that God already knows and that God cares.

But meditation is a simpler, deeper way of praying than words allow; it is a coming to the silent awareness of the indwelling Christ who is our mediator, making all human needs known to the Father through his universal compassion. It is going beyond words, beyond babbling, and through faith coming into the presence of God. This coming to awareness is not something we *do* but something we *are*. And in the silence we find love at the very centre of our *being* and our lives our transformed by this experience and by this discovery.

Different schools of contemplative prayer

One often finds meditators wondering about the relationship of Centering Prayer to Christian Meditation and are there differences in the teaching? Both these spiritual paths follow the hesychastic prayer tradition, which teaches unity of mind and heart and resting in God's silence and stillness. Hesychism as previously mentioned is from a Greek word that means rest or *tranquillity*. Both these schools of prayer are also rooted in the 'apophatic' tradition, which stresses that God cannot be reached through the human intellect, but only through the 'way of divine darkness' when the mind is quiet and at rest. So both Centering Prayer and Christian Meditation are rooted in the same Christian contemplative tradition.

The teaching on Centering Prayer has been developed by two Cistercian monks, Thomas Keating and Basil Pennington.

However while both paths of prayer follow the same general contemplative tradition there are differences in the teaching, particularly the 'intermittent' mantra of Centering Prayer and the continuous recitation of the mantra urged by John Main.

In June 1993 Father Laurence Freeman, Director of the World Community for Christian Meditation, and Father Thomas Keating met at New Harmony, Indiana, USA to discuss the contemplative movement in today's church and to affirm the validity of both of their approaches to the practice of contemplative prayer.

The two communities of meditation remain distinct in their teaching tradition but are collaborative in offering mutual encouragement so that the contemplative renewal throughout the world will continue to grow. Both monks feel the Holy Spirit leads a person towards one or the other path or other spiritual paths as a part of God's unique providence for each individual.

Meditation and other ways of prayer

Christian Meditation is *one* way of prayer but obviously not the *only* way to pray. There are many forms of prayer including vocal prayer, petitionary prayer, liturgical prayer, the prayerful reading of Scripture, the rosary, novenas, Charismatic prayer, the Ignatian exercises and various other forms of devotions and discursive meditation.

However, John Main does point out that the practice of Christian Meditation enhances these other areas of our spiritual life. For instance, the experience of so many people who have begun to meditate is that they develop a hunger and need for the sacramental life. Many meditators also discover a renewed interest in Scripture and its importance. A priest in Ireland once made this statement: 'I had always read Scripture daily in the Divine Office, but it wasn't until after I had started to meditate that Scripture started to leap off the pages at me.'

It is important to note that one who begins to meditate does not have to give up other forms of prayer. Meditation does not preclude praying in any other way. What usually happens is that the daily spiritual discipline of meditation becomes a priority and other forms of prayer take a secondary role in our spiritual life. John Main never said that Christian Meditation is the *only* or even the *best* way of prayer. But in one of his talks in 1976 to the Cistercian monks at Thomas Merton's monastery in Kentucky, he said this:

> As I understand it, all Christian prayer is a growing awareness

of God in Jesus. And for that growing awareness we need to come to a state of undistraction, to a state of attention and concentration – that is, to a state of awareness. And as far as I have been able to determine in the limitations of my own life, the only way that I have been able to find to come to that quiet, to that undistractedness, to that concentration, is the way of the mantra.

In the book *Word Into Silence* he also made this comment:

> I do not wish to imply that meditation is the only way, but rather that it is the only way that I have found. In my own experience it is the way of pure simplicity that enables us to become fully, integrally aware of the Spirit Jesus has sent into our heart; and this is the recorded experience of the mainstream of the Christian tradition from Apostolic times down to our own day.

However the spiritual teacher and author, Father William Johnston sj, says that sooner or later all ways of prayer must lead to that silence wherein one rests in the presence of God. 'All forms of prayer', says Father Johnston in his book *Being in Love*, 'converge finally on contemplative prayer. No matter where you begin, you end with contemplation'.

Meditation and its relationship to the charismatic movement

Father Robert Wild, who helped to start one of the first charismatic prayer groups in Buffalo, New York in 1970, and who is now a member of the Madonna House Community in Combermere, Ontario, Canada, has written two books on the charismatic renewal, *Enthusiasm in the Spirit* and *The Post-Charismatic Experience*. The later book is a very perceptive analysis of where the charismatic movement is heading. The author opines many charismatics are being called to enter into the desert experience and the interior spiritual journey.

Fr Wild says many charismatics now feel the call to a deeper and different kind of spirituality. He writes: 'it will be a spirituality drawn to channel their spiritual energies into deeper silence, more private prayer, a prayer which emphasizes stillness and repose rather than external expression.'

The book – written in 1984 – was prophetic because all around the world we see individual members of charismatic prayer groups now seeking the path of silence and stillness in prayer. All the contemporary evidence points to the charismatic movement open-

CHRISTIAN MEDITATION AND OTHER WAYS

ing itself up to the Christian contemplative tradition. This, of course, does not mean that charismatics must give up their regular charismatic prayer group meetings. The two spiritual paths could go hand in hand. In fact with this cross-fertilisation much needed silence could be introduced into the Charismatic prayer group meetings. A leader in the English charismatic movement, Benedictine monk Benedict Heron, takes this perspective. He feels that charismatics often have contemplative experiences in their prayer meetings. Says Father Heron, 'When I am leading a Charismatic prayer meeting I always try to ensure that there is sufficient time for silence and for listening to the Lord. There needs to be sufficient time for both singing and silence.' Fr Heron also points out

> in our charismatic prayer meetings here we tell them that a fruitful participation in the evening prayer meeting presupposes enough time spent alone with the Lord daily. However we may not always tell them how to spend that time alone with the Lord. I think the John Main tradition of meditation can be the right help for some people there.

John Main had an inkling before he died in 1982 that the Spirit would lead Charismatics to a deeper interior silence in prayer. His hopes are being realised today. Not only John Main but spiritual guides everywhere point out that charismatics must go beyond 'speaking in tongues' to experiencing God in silence and stillness.

Thomas Keating in his book *Intimacy With God* says:

> While baptism in the Spirit does not establish an advanced stage of spiritual development, it is a manifest call to contemplative prayer. The contemplative tradition of the church teaches that contemplative prayer is the normal development of the practice of the Christian life.

Christian and Transcendental Meditation

Transcendental Meditation, or TM, is the name of a worldwide organisation founded by the Maharishi Mahesh Yogi. Needless to say there is often confusion in the public mind whether TM is similar or the same as Christian Meditation. The confusion is understandable because there are a number of outward resemblances between the two traditions. Both demand two daily meditation periods, the same upright sitting position and the use of a mantra to bring the mind to stillness.

Although it teaches mantra meditation in much the same way as originally taught by Father John Main, TM has seemingly distanced itself from its spiritual roots and adapted it primarily as a technique for health, relaxation, well being, business efficiency and relief from stress. High prices are charged to learn the technique and those who join TM are encouraged to 'progress' and to pay for and learn various other practices. The organisation also has political aspirations and has formed its own party to engage in elections in various countries of the world. John Main in *Word Made Flesh* says:

> There can be a real danger that meditation is presented in terms of return and payoff. Most of the books on meditation in the bookshops offer a whole list of returns from lowering your blood pressure to better exam results and levitation. But whether any of these results, some reasonable, some false, occur at all is not of the slightest importance. The only important thing is that your spirit lives, that it lives wholly and that it realises its union with God and with all.

As John Main points out, the spiritual tradition of Christian Meditation – unlike TM – does not have immediate goals in mind. The *Cloud of Unknowing* also says that in this Christian way of prayer we are to lift up our hearts to God in humble love and not for what we can get from God. Christian Meditation is not an escape from pain, suffering, conflict, struggle and darkness but in fact a deliberate embracing of the gospel message that the person who loses their life will save it.

In answering a question on TM in his book *Short Span of Days*, Laurence Freeman points out that what makes meditation for a Christian different as a spiritual path is that it is not practised as a technique. Says Father Laurence,

> There's a world of difference between meditating as a technique and as a discipline. We are technologically conditioned and so we think there is a great technique to discover. We think 'we will use this and see what we get out of it, improve our performance, and we can let go of it if it doesn't pay off.' But as a discipline we bring a dimension of faith and perseverance to meditation. Perhaps we have to practise for some time before we really understand what that faith means. But this is why it is important that meditation is taught as a spiritual discipline rather than merely as a technique.

William Johnston in his book *Being in Love* says 'what makes religious meditation . . . religious (as opposed to the secular meditation practised for the development of human potential) is the dimension of love.' He goes on to point out that the human heart has an infinite capacity for love and this is the love that springs from the depth of the spirit in our life of prayer. However it should be pointed out here that some Christians do discover in TM that it is a spiritual path and some people who have practised TM do join Christian Meditation groups. In addition we should remember that John Main first learned mantra meditation from a Hindu Swami in Malaya which later led him to recover the Christian tradition of mantra meditation. So we owe a great debt to that most ancient spiritual tradition in India which has kept alive the practice and teaching of meditation, and has always been prepared to share it so generously with others. (See Chapter 15 'Christian Meditation and Unity with Other Faiths'.)

TM does lay down a challenge to Christianity. The challenge is to face the question 'Why is the Christian tradition of Meditation the best kept secret in the church today?' If TM, according to the recent newspaper article, can have 20,000 people meditating in Toronto, why are the Christian churches not communicating more effectively the 'good news' about Christian Meditation. The challenge is there to share the gift of John Main's teaching on silence and stillness in prayer with family, friends, colleagues and acquaintances. *Gifts* are meant to be given away.

15
Christian Meditation and unity with other faiths

Every great spiritual tradition has known that the human spirit begins to be aware of its own Source only in profound stillness.

In the Hindu tradition the Upanishads speak of the spirit of the One who created the universe as dwelling in our heart. The same spirit is described as the One who in silence is loving to all.

In our own Christian tradition Jesus tells us that the Spirit who dwells in our heart is the Spirit of love.

(JOHN MAIN, *Moment of Christ*)

The meeting of East and West in the Spirit is one of the great features of our time, but it can only be fruitful if it is realized on the level of deep prayer. This, surely, is also true of the union of the different Christian denominations.

(JOHN MAIN, *Word Into Silence*)

What our encounter with India and the East is teaching us is something we should never have forgotten – that the essential Christian experience is beyond the capacity of any cultural or intellectual form to express or contain. This is what St Paul called the 'glorious liberty of the children of God': no restriction.

This experience has to be restored to the heart of the Church if she is to face creatively the challenge before her: the challenge of the renewal of her contemplative religious life, the challenge of restoring unity in the Spirit with all Christian communions, the challenge of embracing non-Christian religions with the universal love of Christ which is already present in the hearts of all people and which she has a special duty to release and identify. To meet these challenges each one of us must be personally rooted in Jesus' personal experience of God and which he shares with us all through his Spirit.

We do not earn this experience or create it from our own resources; it is for us to prepare for the grace of its giving.

(JOHN MAIN, *Letters From the Heart*)

We meet in the cave of the heart

Silence is a universal value in all the major religions of the world and this contemplative dimension of religion provides a strong base of unity.

At the Second Vatican Council (1965) the church fathers stated:

> Reflect attentively on how Christian religious life may be able to assimilate the ascetic and contemplative traditions whose seeds were sometimes planted by God in ancient cultures prior to the preaching of the Gospel.
>
> (Decree of the church's missionary activity, *Ad Gentes* 18)

Another important statement in this same document from the Vatican Council emphasised that God's divine truth could be found in non-Christian religions:

> The Catholic Church rejects nothing that is true and holy in these religions. She regards with sincere reverence those ways of conduct and of life, those precepts and teachings which, though differing in many respects from the ones she holds and sets forth, nonetheless often reflect a ray of that truth which enlightens all ... Indeed, she proclaims and ever must proclaim Christ 'the way, the truth and the life' (John 14:6) in whom all may find the fullness of religious life, in whom God has reconciled all things ... The Church therefore exhorts her (children) that through dialogue and collaboration with the followers of other religions, carried out with prudence and love, and in witness to the Christian faith and life, they recognize, preserve and promote the good things, spiritual and moral, as well as the socio-cultural values found among these [people].
>
> (Declaration on the relation of the Church to non-Christian religions, *Nostra Aetate* 2)

Dom Bede Griffiths felt strongly that those in the West have much to learn from Eastern forms of contemplative prayer, and this shared experience would bring us into a deeper unity with meditators from other faiths. (See the Life of Bede Griffiths in this chapter.) He pointed out that silence in prayer is at the heart of all true religion and this silence would be the unifying element in any religious dialogue with other faiths. In a 1983 lecture in the USA, Father Bede said: 'What we find is that if you're arguing doctrines and so on, you get nowhere, but when you meet in meditation you begin to share your own inner experience (and) you begin to realize an underlying unity behind the religions.'

Father Bede also felt the Indian scriptures, the Upanishads and the Bhagavad Gita are an immeasurable gift that would enrich the inner life of Westerners. In addition he also felt that the Eastern stress on non-duality would be a reminder that in every religious tradition when you get to the deepest level, there is non-duality, no division, but union with the transcendent. Another unifying aspect of meditation, said Father Bede, would be the problem of how to get beyond the ego, a problem common to every religious tradition including Christianity, Hindu, Buddhist, Muslim, and Judaism.

Ken Wilber in *Grace and Grit* in speaking about meditation echoes this unifying aspect of disciplined silence when he points out that it is part of the universal culture of all humankind. He says:

> Because when you can find a truth that the Hindus and Christians and Buddhists and Taoists and Sufis all agree on, then you have probably found something that is profoundly important, something that tells you about universal truths and ultimate meanings, something that touches the very core of the human condition.

Thomas Merton also felt it important for Christians to acknowledge the genuine tradition of contemplative prayer in other faiths. In *The Inner Experience*, he says:

> Supernatural and mystical contemplation is certainly possible outside the visible church, since God is the master of his gifts and wherever there is sincerity and an earnest desire for truth, He will not deny the gifts of his grace. As we grow in knowledge and appreciation of oriental religion we will come to realize the depth and richness of its varied forms of contemplation.

Perhaps another Benedictine in India, Swami Abhishiktananda, (Henri Le Saux OSB, 1910–1973) put it most succinctly when referring to the unity of those who meditate from different traditions; he said, 'we meet in the Cave of the Heart'.

Beyond East and West

Meditation as a way of prayer bridges both East and West, Orthodox and Latin churches too. John Cassian, who passed on this spiritual tradition of prayer, was a Western monk born in what is today Croatia and ended his life in Marseilles, France (Gaul) after establishing a monastery there. (See Chapter 8 on John Cassian.)

However, we can learn much from Eastern spirituality. Traditionally in the West we have prayed with the head. But the Semitic Eastern approach has taught us to encounter God within our own heart. It has been said that if you ask a Western child where God lives, he will point to the sky. If you ask an Eastern child where God lives, he will point to his own heart. Eastern spirituality has always had an in-depth understanding of John's gospel of the 'indwelling Christ'. In the West we have tended to separate soul and body, matter and spirit. The Eastern approach is to integrate the faculties into a harmonious whole. In Hindu scriptures, the Upanishads, we find God residing 'in the cave of the heart'.

The great gift of Eastern Christian spirituality is the understanding that we cannot reach God conceptually or through a discursive approach of the mind, but only by a loving surrender to God in the depths of our own being. This in effect is a good definition of this path of Christian Meditation.

Bede Griffiths and the spiritual bridge between the world's religions

Dom Bede Griffiths died 13 May 1993 at the ashram of Shantivanam in southern India at the age of 87. He was an internationally respected spiritual teacher who devoted his life to the integration of Christian, Hindu and Buddhist spiritual traditions and to the development of the path of contemplative prayer. In his introduction to the book, *The Inner Christ*, he made the statement that 'in my experience John Main is the best spiritual guide in the church to-day'. I am grateful to Father Laurence Freeman for his reflections on Father Bede's life which follow:

> In his autobiography *The Golden String*, published at the midpoint of his life, Bede Griffiths described his attempt to live a life of radical simplicity with two companions in a Cotswolds cottage in England after they left Oxford in 1929. It led him to a spiritual and psychological crisis which in turn led from a worship of Romance and Reason to an experience of God, to becoming a Catholic and in 1933 to entering Prinknash Abbey as a Benedictine monk.
>
> The last years of his long life were lived in a simple hut beside the River Kauvery, the sacred river of South India, in his Benedictine ashram of Shantivanam. In a way his life had come full circle. The ideal of a small self-sufficient contemplative community had been realised but it had also become one of the world's great centres of inter-faith dialogue and prayer. It drew thousands of visitors each year, including many meditators.
>
> Through extensive travels in America, Europe and Australia in his later years, Fr Bede developed the vision of modern life and religion which is his abiding legacy. He saw the modern

world at a crossroads comparable to only two or three such epochs in human history. And he saw the recovery of a spiritual vision as an essential means for its survival. The sometimes exclusive claims and dualistic thinking of the Semitic religions of Judaism, Christianity and Islam, which had been responsible for so many wars and so much hatred, needed, he believed, to be touched by the *advaita* or non-dualism and the contemplative priority of experience of the Asian religions. This idea was developed brilliantly in his 1982 book *A Marriage of East and West*.

The deepest source of his vision was his own spiritual path of meditation. From the 1940s he had practised the Jesus Prayer, a form of the interior and non-discursive prayer of the heart which he saw as an essential complement to all the forms of external worship. In the teachings of the Christian tradition of meditation by his fellow Benedictine John Main (1926–1982) he discovered meditation and the way of the mantra as an essential bridge between East and West.

At the John Main Seminar which he led at New Harmony, Indiana in 1991 he used John Main's thought to crystallise his own vision of prayer and contemporary spiritual needs, particularly the need for community. These Seminar talks were published as *The New Creation in Christ* and describe his profound sense of the crisis facing modern humanity, but also his sense of hope and faith.

Bede Griffiths is one of the great religious prophets of modern times. His influence will continue to be felt not only in those he has inspired but through the writings he has left to be published after his death. He testifies to the possibility, rarely achieved in a sceptical age, of uniting intellect with spirit and of their integration in a human nature of great gentleness and profound compassion for others, through all the adventures of a long life of seeking and sharing God.

16
Meditation and action – both sides of the same coin

> *It often seems to many people that prayer is an introspective state and that the meditator is someone going into oneself to the exclusion of people and creation around them. Nothing could be further from the truth . . . Because meditation leads us into the actual experience of love at the centre of our being, it necessarily makes us more loving people in our ordinary lives and relationships.*
>
> (JOHN MAIN, *Letters From the Heart*)

> *If our life is rooted in Christ, rooted in his love and the conscious knowledge of his love, then we need have no anxiety about regulating our action. Our action will always spring from and be informed and shaped by that love. Indeed, the more active we are, the more important it is that our action springs from and is grounded in contemplation. And contemplation means deep, silent, communion; knowing who we are. Knowing who we are by being who we are. That we are rooted and founded in Christ, the Resurrection of God, is Christian self-knowledge.*
>
> (JOHN MAIN, *The Way of Unknowing*)

The inner eye of love

One woman recently said to a meditator, 'I just don't trust that meditation business. All you meditators do is sit in a cave and contemplate your belly button while the rest of the world goes hungry.' All of us who are meditating one time or another, usually have to face those who are often suspicious and mistrustful of what is happening to us on the meditative journey. People often look to see if we are using prayer as an escape from our life and responsibilities.

John Main was quite adamant that meditation, *far* from being an escape from life, actually propels one *into* life and to love and compassion for others. Another teacher, the Jesuit Father William Johnston in *Silent Music* also faces this problem head on when he says:

In the final analysis meditation is a love affair. And love is the most powerful energy in the universe. The great irony of meditation is that we become *more* immersed in the here-and-now. When we are liberated from our false egos, we begin to know and love others at a deeper level of awareness. We reach out with a new found compassion to our family, friends, the less fortunate.

The personal fruits of prayer that St Paul talks about can also include a call to action. As Father Johnston points out, the flame of love that springs from prayer can suddenly burst forth. Like the prophets of old, the person who meditates often has an inner eye awakened to suffering and injustice in the world and suddenly discovers that he or she cannot refuse the call to action. The path of meditation often leads to a compassion for the poor, the sick, the oppressed, the weak, the underprivileged, the needy.

We see this in Mother Teresa and Jean Vanier who are involved in the conflicts, suffering, the anguish of the world in which they live and yet are committed to this affirmation of silence in prayer. And apart from these great spiritual witnesses there are a host of meditators around the world who integrate their daily meditation with love, commitment and service to family and community.

Our prayer life and our actions cannot be separated for they are of the same fabric. Prayer and action are both sides of the same coin. This mixed life of prayer and action was chosen by Jesus himself who taught and preached and healed while at the same time devoting so much time to prayer.

For all of us who are meditating it is important to remember that we cannot enjoy the silence and stillness while ignoring our worldly or family affairs and responsibilities. That would simply be a delusion. On the other hand meditation will give us the spiritual energy to change the world. The great seventeenth-century spiritual guide, Father Louis Lallemant said that a person of prayer will accomplish more in one year than another person who does not pray will accomplish in an entire lifetime.

In meditation there is an awakening of the inner eye, the eye of the heart, the inner eye of love. This is the *metanoia* or conversion that is beautifully described in Ezekiel (36:26, 27). 'A new heart I will give you and a new spirit I will put within you; and I will take out of your flesh the heart of stone . . . and I will put my spirit within you.' This is the gospel cry of Jesus: 'change your hearts for the kingdom of heaven is at hand' (Matt. 3:2). On the journey of meditation the inner eye of love transforms our hearts and we are led into a life of fruitful action. For without prayer our actions can often be very sterile. Perhaps St Teresa of Avila said it most succinctly: 'this is the reason for prayer, my daughters, the birth always of good works, good works.' Meditation will never lead us into a selfish preoccupation with ourselves.

Thomas Merton also joins the chorus of those who feel strongly about the necessity of our prayer life overflowing into love and action. He is quoted in *Thomas Merton on Prayer* as saying: 'True prayer must lead us outwards to others.' Merton emphasises this when he says that if we experience God in silent prayer, we experience him not for ourselves alone but also for others. As Merton saw it, contemplation, at its highest intensity, becomes a reservoir of spiritual vitality that pours itself out in the most varied kinds of social involvement.

Buddhists also see clearly the connection between meditation and compassion for others. Joseph Goldstein, a Buddhist teacher of meditation in *Insight Meditation, the Practice of Freedom* says:

> Over a period of time, meditation develops a tremendous tenderness of heart . . . a softening of the mind and heart takes place that transforms the way we relate to ourselves and to others. We begin to feel more deeply and this depth of feeling becomes the wellspring of compassion.

Father Henri Nouwen, the priest-author, who works at a L'Arche House in Ontario, says contemplatives are not the ones who withdraw from the world to save their own soul, but rather the ones who enter into the centre of the world and work and pray there.

A life of meditation presupposes justice and compassion for others. And in fact our social concern for justice and compassion will inevitably keep us on the path of meditation. There is the temptation for some social activists to neglect the interior life and thus open themselves to frustration and burn-out. There is always a *balance* needed between meditation and action.

This integration of prayer and action in the life of Jesus is beautifully described in the Gospel of Mark, 1:35–38.

> In the morning, while it was still very dark, Jesus got up and went out to a deserted place, and there he prayed. And Simon and his companions hunted for him. When they found him, they said to him, 'Everyone is searching for you.'
> He answered, 'Let us go on to the neighbouring towns, so that I may proclaim the message there also; for that is what I came out to do.'

Meister Eckhart warns meditators about divorcing themselves from the world around them. He says that once we find silence we must not ignore our day-to-day affairs and responsibilities. Eckhart reminds us that the external world also is real and has its rights.

God is present in both worlds and we have to learn to find him in both. God is present to us everywhere, says Eckhart, both in and out of silent prayer. A good point to ponder.

Like Eckhart, the contemplative approaching the twenty-first century is also coming to a realisation that God is present in his creation. This incarnational spirituality sees with the eyes of the poet Gerard Manley Hopkins that 'the world is charged with the grandeur of God'. This means a concern for the environment that seeks and finds God in all created things.

Love of silence and compassion for others

One is often asked about examples of well-known individuals who combine love of silence with love, service and compassion to others in their daily life. Two people, of course, come immediately to mind, Mother Teresa, foundress of the Missionaries of Charity and Jean Vanier, founder of the l'Arche community for the mentally challenged.

Mother Teresa has had a lifetime commitment to silence and stillness in prayer combined with an extraordinary service and compassion to the most needy of this world. She has a deep understanding of the relationship between contemplative prayer and action and has ensured that twice-daily times of silent prayer are an integral part of the morning and evening schedule of her sisters.

Here are just a few of her quotes on the relationship of prayer and action and the importance of silence taken from her book *Mother Teresa, Contemplative at the Heart of the World*.

- The more we receive in our silent prayer, the more we can give in our active life.
- Jesus is always waiting for us in silence; it is there that he speaks to our souls.
- God is the friend of silence. See how nature, the trees, the flowers, the grass grow in deep silence. See how the stars, the moon and the sun move in silence.
- Silence gives us a new way of looking at everything. We need this silence in order to touch souls. The essential thing is not what we say (in our active life) but what God says to us and what he says through us.
- We (missionaries of charity) are called to be contemplatives in the world.

Jean Vanier and his family have had a long commitment to the path of silence in prayer. In the biography of Jean's mother entitled *One Woman's Journey*, the authors recount the weekly Christian

MEDITATION AND ACTION

Meditation group led by Pauline Vanier at the L'Arche Community in France. Pauline Vanier played John Main tapes and attracted L'Arche Community members in training from around the world to her weekly group meetings.

Jean Vanier founded L'Arche 30 years ago in August 1964 in Trosly-Breuil, France. Today there are about 200 mentally challenged men and women and 200 assistants living in 20 houses in and around this small French village. In addition there are over 100 L'Arche Communities around the world. Jean gave the 1992 John Main seminar in London, England, and offered his advice and expertise in developing the Constitution for the World Community for Christian Meditation.

The activity in L'Arche Communities flows increasingly from prayer. Jean Vanier has indicated he would be happy to see Christian Meditation groups started in L'Arche houses. Two such communities in Kerala, India and Edmonton, Canada, have subsequently started Christian Meditation groups. Here are a few of Jean Vanier's quotes from his talks about silence in prayer.

- Prayer is to be in contact with our own Centre. It is to let Jesus make his home in us and to make our home in him.
- A spiritual life ... is especially necessary for the weak ... the mentally handicapped ... in love, fraternity, prayer and silence. Their religious life will not primarily be one of action but rather that of contemplation, that is the life of one ... who receives peace and radiates it and who lives a life nourished by prayer.
- When we live in community and everyday life is busy and difficult, it is absolutely essential for us to have moments alone to pray and meet God in silence and quietness.
- Prayer is like a secret garden made up of silence and rest and inwardness.

The fruits of prayer

Concrete examples of the relationship between Christian Meditation and love and compassion for others abound. Here are two stories about the inner transformation that takes place on the journey of meditation.

A mother of five children in New York City tells this story. When she first decided she wanted to meditate she knew she would need her husband's support. However her husband was quite unsympathetic to his wife's desire to 'run away and hide' for two half-hour periods of meditation each day. He thought it was one of his wife's strange quirks. However she was very quick-thinking and she said to him 'look, I'll babysit while you watch the NFL (National Football League) games on Sunday if you'll babysit for my two daily periods of meditation'. So they came to an agreement.

A year after she had been meditating her husband came down to the breakfast table one morning and suddenly said to her 'I think I'll start meditating with you'. In telling this story the woman said 'when I picked myself off the kitchen floor in complete shock I said to him, "what's happened here, you've never shown any interest in meditation before" '. He replied 'you've changed since you've begun to meditate. I notice you're more kind and patient with the children and myself. I've also observed you are giving yourself more to others.' She had joined as a volunteer at a suicide prevention telephone answering service. Then he made the most significant remark of all: 'I don't want you to change any more without me changing with you.'

There is another story, which concerns John Main giving a talk to a group of meditators in Los Angeles. He was talking about the 'harvest of the Spirit', the fruits of prayer as outlined by St Paul: love, joy, peace, *patience*, kindness, goodness, fidelity, gentleness and *self-control* (Gal. 5:22). A meditator during the question and answer period pointed out that he had been meditating for a year and there had been absolutely no fruits of prayer in his life whatsoever. Father John interjected 'none at all?' 'Well', the man replied, after some thought, 'there was a little thing happened on the way here this morning. I drove off the freeway and came to a stoplight. Whereupon a car full of teenagers rammed me from behind. In former years before starting to meditate, I probably would have beaten up the driver. Instead today I got slowly out of the car, walked up to the driver and said, "I think we have a *slight* problem here".'

In telling the story Father John smilingly pointed out that the gentleman in question had undergone a transformation that was greater than any temporary spiritual gifts he might receive during a lifetime. That small act of self-control and patience was the 'fruit' of his prayer life, said Father John, the very fruits of prayer that St Paul talks about.

Escaping or encountering reality

In meditation we discover the only ultimate reality, which is God. But of course there is another reality all around us, the everyday world of politics, economics, hunger, suffering in its many forms, the family, the local community and the emotional and physical needs of our neighbour. Meister Eckhart says this is reality too and that we find God not only in our own heart but also in the real world around us. The practice of Christian Meditation is not an escape from this everyday life but in fact meditation compels us to love, service and compassion for others. In fact the ascesis required on the path of meditation brings us down to earth and to this real world around us. There is a Zen meditation story which illustrates this point. One disciple said: 'My master stands on one side of the river. I stand on the other holding a piece of paper. He draws a picture in the air and the picture appears on my paper. He works miracles.' The other disciple said: 'My master works greater miracles than that.'

> When he sleeps, he sleeps.
> When he eats, he eats.
> When he works, he works.
> When he meditates, he meditates.

There is also another story told by the Buddha, which illustrates the same point. A delegation was once sent to the Buddha and asked him, 'Who are you? Are you a god?' 'I am not,' he replied. 'Well then, are you an angel?' 'I am not.' 'Are you a prophet?' they persisted. 'No,' he replied. 'Who then are you?' they asked. The Buddha replied 'I am awake'.

These stories illustrate a profound point about meditation, namely that its practice opens our eyes and ears to the world of reality around us and this gentle transformation keeps our feet firmly on 'terra firma'. We may enter the 'cave of the heart' in meditation but we do not enter a Himalayan cave. We simply cannot find God in isolation from other human beings. The real meditator takes an interest in the world, keeps abreast of human developments and certainly does not bury ostrich-like his or her head in the sand.

Our selfless relationships in our daily life are the true test of our meditative life. Active virtue and good works overflow from the spiritual discipline of silence in prayer. In fact the person who meditates should be even more interested in what is going on in the world, precisely because they are meditating. There is something incomplete if the love that flows from meditation is not shared. Father William Shannon in the book *Thomas Merton's Dark Path* says: 'that is why heaven, where the ultimate perfection of contemplation will be achieved, will not be a place of separate individuals, each with his own private vision of God; rather it will be a sea of love flowing through the One Person of all the elect.'

Meditation is an experience in aloneness but it is not an experience in isolation. Silence leads one to God and simultaneously outwards to other human beings.

17
From brokenness to wholeness – on the path of meditation

Meditation does restore us to a deeper harmony of body and spirit, but it always remains an essentially spiritual growth. All growth is a form of healing. Not just a retrospective healing of past wounds but it propels the whole person we are now into greater wholeness, the health we are created for. And so we can say that meditation is a growth beyond limitations.

(JOHN MAIN, *The Present Christ*)

Interior silence – the inner stillness to which meditation leads, is where the Spirit secretly anoints the soul and heals our deepest wounds.

(John of the Cross)

A time for inner healing

One important aspect of our spiritual journey is an ongoing reconciliation with the shadow side of our unconscious. We are all wounded in one way or another. We all need inner healing. In the regular practice of Christian Meditation the silence and stillness and the deep rest created by our mantra begins to heal the emotional hurts of our early childhood. The shadow side of the psyche begins to heal.

Some people have a deep ambivalence toward their mother or father. They harbour deep resentment arising from neglect, maltreatment and sometimes even sexual abuse. These are wounds in the psyche and they continue to afflict us unless they are released from our unconscious. Today we are recognising more and more some of the terrible things that children suffer in infancy.

Perhaps the best way to demonstrate the healing aspects of Christian Meditation is to tell the story of Cuan Mhuire and the work at Galilee House in Athy, County Kildare, Ireland.

Fr Pat Murray and Sr Consilio Fitzgerald, both committed to John Main's teaching on the Christian tradition of the mantra, are doing the seemingly impossible. They have taken the most *wounded and broken*, including alcoholics, drug addicts and those suffering from severe depression and have founded four therapeutic communities in Ireland. Called *Cuan Mhuire* in Gaelic, in English it means 'the harbour of many'. The five centres treating over 300 persons are located in Athy (two houses) in County Kildare, Bruree in County Limerick and Newry in County Down plus one in Galway (1994).

Sister Consilio, a sister of Mercy, started her work with alcoholics 30 years ago while working at a hospital in Athy. From a small shack on the grounds where she served tea and 'listened', her apostolate spread over the years to include three large community houses. A few years ago she joined forces with Fr Pat Murray, a Pallottine father, who had a similar commitment and vision and together they have founded a house in Athy called Galilee based on John Main's *Community of Love*. Fr Murray spent seven months with John Main at the Montreal Priory in 1981–82. Galilee House is a House of Prayer and a Home for Growth. Simply stated, it is about the restoration and reconstruction of individual persons.

According to Fr Pat the rehabilitation process of Galilee is directly related to the healing that flows from the three periods of Christian meditation at the house each day. At 9.30 am, 3.30 pm and 7.00 pm everyone gathers to listen to a taped talk by John Main followed by a half hour of silent meditation. The divine office is also recited in the morning and evening. The meditation room in Athy has 40 chairs and meditation stools, and a plaque dedicates the room to the memory of John Main. Another plaque outlines the *how to* of meditation.

In addition to the spiritual programme, those who come to Galilee participate in two daily therapeutic sessions where each person is urged to take their life in their own hands and through the support of others say *yes* to life. According to Fr Pat, this inner transformation primarily comes about through the daily discipline of the mantra. Says Fr Pat:

> Our periods of meditation and our actions . . . the two cannot be separated. How well we care for others is as much a part of meditation as what we do in the stillness and silence. That is why all our staff meditate as well as our patients. True prayer becomes a reservoir of love that pours itself out in the service of others.

In discussions with Father Pat and Sister Consilio they have pointed out that most of the people referred to Cuan Mhuire have suppressed anger, or buried resentment and often have suffered a lack of forgiveness in their lives; all neuroses and hurts says Fr Pat, which have generally existed in their unconscious since early childhood or adolescence. Many have suffered childhood abuse. Quite often, he pointed out, these wounds go back to a neurotic relationship with one's parents that unfortunately can cripple us emotionally. The need to exist as the persons they were meant to be was frustrated, says Fr Pat, due to the lack of a loving and human environment. The need to be seen, heard, believed, recognised and feel safe and secure was frustrated in some way. Hence, they feel ashamed, fearful, guilty or continuously rebellious in some way.

Father Pat is very unequivocal that while the psychotherapy is somewhat helpful, the real reason why patients heal in this programme is meditation. He put it succinctly: 'When people come into contact with *the* healer they begin to heal.' And he explained further that 'In the silence of meditation, God who is love, penetrates to the buried unconscious, allowing the suppressed hurt to surface and to be healed'. 'Exposed to the light', he said, 'neuroses begin to melt away.' The healing power of Christ, he says, drains the poisoned memories away.

He also pointed out that while meditation does not wipe out the memory, the memory loses its power over us. Once these memories have been identified and brought to the light, says Fr Pat, Christ frees us from the crippling effects of what we had buried in our unconscious and he brings an inner healing. He added that 'In meditation we come to accept ourselves as we are. And this self-acceptance is the first great key to integration of the personality and healing.'

In meditation says Fr Pat we come to an experiential conviction that we are loved by another person, profoundly loved. We understand deeply that it is *not* that I love but that I *am* loved. Through this acceptance of the gift of love we grow from childhood to adulthood. In this healing process of meditation, he reiterates, neuroses and hang-ups of all kinds melt away before the infinite, gentle energy of lovingly saying each syllable of the mantra in the *now*.

Now what is the process that leads to this inner healing, the healing of the wounded sensibility, the healing of hurts? As Fr Pat points out it is simply the saying of our mantra in meditation which opens us to the healing of love. In the silence of meditation God reaches down into the depths and liberates us little by little from the emotional damage of a lifetime. There is an organic unfolding in their own time of our buried neuroses.

In meditation, says Fr Pat, our conscious level is swept clean so that the unconscious can surface. In meditation our pain is identified and brought into the light. The healing process of Christian

Meditation can then begin. This is the path, says Fr Pat that leads from brokenness to wholeness.

How do we know that we are healed? We can recognise this when the disproportionate and recurring reactions related to the pain have disappeared. And the recollection of the traumatic events, whether it be expressed or not, leaves not even a trace of painful or lasting sensations of any kind.

'In my experience', says Fr Pat, 'meditation is one of the greatest means, that I know of, in the healing process of past traumas.'

One other excellent resource available on the subject of 'brokenness to wholeness' are the cassette tapes available of the 1992 John Main Seminar given by Jean Vanier and available from the World Community for Christian Meditation (Medio Media) and its distributors around the world. (See Chapter 21 on the role of the World Community for Christian Meditation.)

The woman at the well

> *A woman of Samaria came to draw water. Jesus said to her, 'Give me a drink'. His disciples had gone into the town to buy food.*
>
> *The Samaritan woman said to him, 'How can you, a Jew, ask me, a Samaritan woman, for a drink?' (For Jews use no utensils in common with Samaritans.) Jesus answered and said to her, 'If you but knew the gift of God and who is saying to you, "Give me a drink", you would have asked him and he would have given you living water.'*
>
> *[The woman] said to him, 'Sir you do not even have a bucket and the cistern is deep; where then can you get this living water? Are you greater than our Father Jacob, who gave us this cistern and drank from it himself with his children and his flocks?'*
>
> *Jesus answered and said to her, 'Everyone who drinks this water will be thirsty again; but whoever drinks the water I shall give will never thirst; the water I shall give will become a spring of water welling up to eternal life.' The woman said to him, 'Sir, give me this water, so that I may not be thirsty or have to keep coming here to draw water.'*
>
> (John 4:7–15)

Jesus says 'If you but know the gift of God, you would have living water, a spring of water welling up into eternal life'. John identifies this river of living water as the Holy Spirit. But Thomas Merton points out that the words 'living waters' is a term that has always been used by spiritual writers to describe the silence of the contemplative path of prayer. Merton writes in *The Waters of Siloe*:

> There is intoxication in the waters of contemplation, whose mystery fascinated and delighted the first Cistercians and their

monasteries that stood on the banks of clean streams, among rocks alive with springs.

These are the waters which the world does not know, because it prefers the water of bitterness and contradiction. These are the waters of peace, of which Christ said: 'The one that shall drink of the water that I shall give, shall not thirst forever. But the water that I shall give shall become a fountain of water, springing up into life everlasting.'

These are the waters, says Merton, that flow in silence.

In this meeting at the well each one of us must become the Samaritan woman. We, all of us, in some way or another, are broken, wounded as she was. But God asks us to drink. He issues the invitation. And his living water flows in silence – the gift of meditation. We can refuse the gift or accept it. The decision is ours. But the invitation is there. The knock on the door is there.

There is a deep symbolism for all of us who meditate in the story of the woman at the well. Jesus in this story is the healer and a God of tremendous love. And the Samaritan woman is really in each one of us. We, as she was, are often in pain, broken, wounded, longing to experience ourselves as loved and loveable. And Jesus says to her and to us 'If you but knew the gift of God'. But in our daily periods of meditation we do come to experience this gift of God.

In our fidelity to silence in prayer, Jesus progressively reveals himself and his love to us. In our commitment to the path of meditation our woundedness is healed, we are changed and we are transformed. But this change, this transformation is never easy. Jean Vanier talked eloquently about this transformation at the 1991 John Main Seminar in London, England.

And of course we do not want to change. We like to stay where we are because to change is to die, to die to our ego, our false self. On starting off on the pilgrimage of meditation we cling to what is familiar and dread the journey to what is unfamiliar. We hesitate to give up words, images, our imagination and simply sit before the Lord in silence. We would rather keep babbling on. That is why John Main says meditation at times requires courage and in the final analysis is a path of pure faith. In meditation Jesus wants us to walk on the path of insecurity so that we can discover that he in fact is our security.

Jesus could say to each one of us 'If you but knew the gift of God. Of how much I want to love you, of how I want to transform you through the path of silence and stillness in prayer . . . of how I want you to become filled and overflow with living waters of love and compassion for others.'

Jesus looked at that woman of Samaria as he looks at us with eyes of love. No judgement, no condemnation. He was saying in effect, as he says to us, 'If you but knew how much I love you just as you are.' Perhaps it's only when we touch the depths of our poverty, the poverty of the mantra in our times of meditation, that we begin to experience real love.

At a talk at the 1992 John Main Seminar, Jean Vanier pointed out that, like the Samaritan woman, we cannot deny our own brokenness, our weaknesses, our flaws. But Jesus is gentle, he does not condemn us, criticise us, crush us. In meditation he simply puts his finger on our wounds and we begin to heal. We stop running away and open ourselves to our vulnerability as the Samaritan woman did. Meditation teaches us not to pretend we are not wounded, but to accept our brokenness. Not to pretend that everything is OK but to open ourselves to forgiveness. In meditation we discover, like the Samaritan woman, that we are loved unconditionally. We discover that we are held in the hands of a God of incredible love.

So meditation has this power that heals us. The very word *meditation* and the word *medicine* come from the same root. Medicine refers to that which heals the physical; and meditation heals the spiritual. Both have healing power. And just as Jesus healed the Samaritan woman at the well, so we are healed by his presence in meditation. To be healed simply means to be made whole and to be integrated.

And so he speaks to each one of us when he says 'If you but knew the gift of God and who it is who is speaking to you, you would have asked to drink and I would have given you rivers of living water.' You just have to ask for it.

In the silence of meditation we, in fact, become a well . . . this spring of living water. These are the waters of peace of which Christ said, 'The one that shall drink of the water that I shall give, shall never thirst again. But the water that I shall give shall become a fountain of water, springing up into life everlasting' (John 4:14–15).

18
Commitment and perseverance on the path of meditation

There are no half measures. You can't decide to do a bit of meditation. The option is to meditate and to root your life in reality. As far as I can understand it, that is what the Gospel is about. That is what Christian prayer is about. A commitment to life, a commitment to eternal life. As Jesus himself put it, the Kingdom of heaven is here and now, what we have to do is to be open to it, which is to be committed to it.

A way of limitless life requires on our part openness, generosity and simplicity. Above all, it requires commitment. Not commitment to a cause or ideology but commitment in our own lives to the simplicity of the daily return to the roots of our own existence, a commitment to respond to life with attention, to create the space in our own lives to live fully. What we learn in meditation, in the silence of it and in the simplicity of it, is that we have nothing to fear from the commitment to creating this space.

I think all of us fear commitment because it seems to be a reducing of our options. We say to ourselves, 'Well, if I commit myself to meditating, then I'll not be able to do other things.' But I think what all of us find is that this fear dissolves in the actual commitment to be serious, to be open, to love not out of the shallows of our being, but out of its depths. What we all find in the experience of meditation is that our horizons are expanding, not contracting, and we find, not constraint, but liberty.

(JOHN MAIN, *Moment of Christ*)

The desert experience

On our meditative pilgrimage there seem to be three stages of growth. The first stage is called *conversion*. It is that initial enthusiasm and commitment that we give to our daily periods of meditation as we start off on the journey. The second stage of growth is an ever deepening *discipline* where we get down to our daily practice without demands for any 'results' whatsoever. It sometimes takes a long time to get to this stage. We are so conditioned in our society and in our lives to seeing some results from efforts exerted. But this second stage demands an indifference to what happens in our daily periods of meditation. We are indifferent to distractions or silence. We look for no 'results'. We simply stand before the Lord each day in our times of prayer and make no demands. We have no expectations.

The spiritual journey

In our spiritual journey there can also be a period of aridity, of turbulence, of distractions, of nothingness where God seems to have disappeared. We cannot find him. He seems to have left us. This stage of the journey is our time in the desert or wilderness.

St John of the Cross calls it the 'dark night of the soul'. He says it is a time where there is no consolation of any kind, where we feel deserted by God. He terms it a sensory dark night of purgation. In the *Dark Night* he writes: 'When God sees that they (souls) have grown a little, he weans them from the sweet breast so that they might be strengthened, lays aside their swaddling bands, and puts them down from his arms that they may grow accustomed to walking by themselves.'

There are four short quotations that are so pertinent to the desert. The first is from the New Testament. St Luke says (5:16) referring to Jesus, 'but he himself retired to the desert and prayed there'. The second is from Hosea in the Old Testament. Hosea (2:16), God says 'I will lead you to the desert and speak to your heart'. The third quotation is from Thomas Merton who said, 'Contemplative prayer is simply the preference for the desert, for emptiness, for poverty'. And the final quotation is by Father Robert Wild, who has written in *The Post-Charismatic Experience*: 'God is in the desert. Don't be afraid to enter there. He really cannot be found any place else . . . He loves you and awaits in the desert to embrace you and lead you home.'

The desert in Scripture

The desert has always had a special meaning and role in both the Old and New Testaments. It has always been a place where people retreated when they sought solitude, silence and closeness to God.

Charles Cummings, a Cistercian monk, is the author of the book *Spirituality and the Desert Experience*, and I am indebted for many

COMMITMENT AND PERSEVERANCE

of his insights in attempting to answer this question about the relationship of meditation to the desert experience.

For those on the meditative path the term 'desert experience' refers to our inner journey of prayer where one begins to 'let go' of attachments, where the desert becomes an instrument of transformation. An inner path that leads to freedom, peace, love and joy. The secret of surviving and even of flourishing in the desert is a loving trust and faith in the Lord. In the desert experience of meditation we will discover a special intimacy and nearness to God. In the desert we experience God in a new way.

Yet there is a great paradox here says Father Cummings. The desert experience is generally a time of purification, cleansing and pruning. The desert experience means an emptying of our self-centredness. For those on the path of meditation the desert experience often means aridity and dryness, the feeling of boredom, and even the sense of being abandoned by God. We are no longer aware of God's loving presence in our daily times of meditation. It especially can be a time of endless distractions in meditation when interior silence seems very far away. One contemporary meditator has put the desert experience in modern terms: 'God seems a billion light years away. He has simply disappeared. He is inexplicably absent.' There is certainly an absence of consolations in the desert.

Thomas Merton in talking about the desert says,

> The prospect of this wilderness is something that so appals most people that they refuse to enter upon its burning sands and travel among its rocks. They cannot believe that contemplation and sanctity are to be found in a desolation where there is no food and no shelter and no refreshment for their imagination and intellect and the desires of their nature.

In our personal life the desert experience can be a time of trauma, loss of a loved one, sickness, emotional or physical suffering, loneliness, separation, divorce, difficulties in our work situation, the physical problems of old age. Personal difficulties can lead us into the desert.

As Jesus was tempted in the desert so we will also be tempted. Again the desert is a time of spiritual testing. In the desert of emptiness and dryness and the feeling that God is absent, we can be tempted to skip our meditation periods. We can rationalise that we will make it up later, that we are not in the right mood for meditation . . . that we need to devote ourselves to some apostolic action or 'good works'. Behind our rationalisation lies a feeling of resentment. We are hurt. God seems to have let us down. We rationalise and say to ourselves 'If I am generous enough to give God two half hours of my time in meditation each day, He could at least give me a little encouragement'. This is the self-analysis and self-questioning of our meditation that John Main begs us to avoid. This is the self concern we are meant to leave behind in meditation.

Meditation and the desert experience

John Main knew full well that there is nothing we can do to force God to reveal himself to us. Only faith – as practised in the faithful repetition and the acceptance of the poverty of the mantra will save us. The Israelites had to spend 40 years in the desert learning the lesson that there was very little they could do to save themselves; the situation was fundamentally beyond their control and they had to place all their trust in a God who would provide for them and lead them on one day at a time.

In our own desert experience and in the poverty and emptiness of meditation we too have to learn to accept our state of helplessness and nothingness so that God can fill us with himself. Thomas Merton puts this paradox so well. He says 'only when we are able to "let go" of everything within us, all desire to see, to know, to taste and to experience the consolation of God, only then are we truly able to experience that presence'.

The desert experience in meditation tells us that we have to trust that God is present and that he loves us even when he seems permanently absent. Until he comes to deliver us we have to go on persevering in our periods of meditation. God follows his own timetable in the desert experience.

The desert experience challenges us to overcome our self-centredness. Can we meditate without concern for where God is leading us? Can we meditate faithfully when distractions bombard us? Can we meditate when nothing 'happens' in meditation? Can we give up our desire to possess God and shed all desire or spiritual consolation in meditation?

Can we meditate with ever deepening generosity and commitment? Our faith will never be pure if we cannot. And so the desert purifies our motives. The desert challenges us to forget about ourselves in prayer. The desert eats away at our self-centredness. Again the desert is a place where we are tempted and tested, brought to self-knowledge, purified and strengthened through faith.

In the desert, says Father Cummings, we always prefer the easy way, the path of least suffering. We prefer, of course, to be in the promised land and not in the desert. Satan also offered Jesus the promised land of plenty, but Jesus preferred the desert until

COMMITMENT AND PERSEVERANCE

God's spirit should lead him elsewhere. The desert is God's way to the promised land – union with him. In our meditative journey we must come to love the desert because it is a way of placing ourselves in God's hands with confidence and trust. The meditator lives by trusting and obeying God in the desert of doubt, temptation, boredom, aridity and distraction.

The desert as a place of beauty

But there is a great paradox about the desert experience. The desert can also be a place of beauty, of rest, of peace. A place where we can hear God in the silence of our own heart, where at times we can remotely sense his presence, where our eyes are beginning to open. With our fidelity to meditation we will come to love the desert.

God looked after the Israelites in the desert and fed them with food from heaven. The desert is not a place of sadness. It can be a place of great joy. There are flowers between the sand and the rocks, there are living things, there is beauty. God lives in the desert and leads us. The desert experience may seem like it lasts for a long time, but salvation history assures us the desert does not last forever.

> The wilderness and the dry land shall be glad,
>   the desert shall rejoice and blossom;
> like the crocus it shall blossom abundantly,
>   and rejoice with joy and singing.
>
> (Isa. 35:1–4)

God guides us through the desert. He will never permit us to be tried beyond our strength, or to experience desertedness and emptiness beyond the limits of our endurance. It is by the power of God's grace and his Holy Spirit present in us that we can say 'yes' to his apparent absence in our desert experience.

Joy in the desert

The paradox is that our feelings of loneliness and inner emptiness in the desert can simultaneously coexist in our hearts along with a deep peace, joy and a sense of humour. In the desert we can have a compassionate love and a transforming hope and joy in the risen Christ dwelling within us. Life goes on in the desert.

But more than that we are invited to *intimacy* in the desert. God invites us in the Song of Songs to enter into a deeper life with him. And in this new life of the Spirit there is refreshment and joy.

Come then, my love
My lovely one, come.
For see, winter is past,
The rains are over and gone.
The flowers appear on the earth,
The season of glad songs has come,
The cooing of the turtledoves is heard in our land.

(Song 2:10–12)

To climb the mountain of the Lord

The geographical pilgrimage is the symbolic acting out of an interior journey.

(THOMAS MERTON, *Mystics and Zen Masters*)

A highway will be there
called the holy way
It is for those with a journey to make
and on it the redeemed will walk.

(Isa. 35:8–9)

In days to come
The mountain of the Lord's house
shall be established as the highest mountain
and raised above the hills
All nations shall stream toward it
many peoples shall come and say

Come, let us climb the Lord's mountain
to the house of the God of Jacob
That he may instruct us in his ways,
and we may walk in his paths.

(Isa. 2:2–4)

A few years ago in Cumbria, like thousands of others over the years, I hiked from Brotherswater Lake up to Hart and Dove Crags (2,698 ft). A guide to the Eastern fells describes Dove Crag as 'one of the most impressive cliffs in England'. For six days I had climbed the beautiful Cumbrian hills, up to the Hayeswater, Green Hill overlooking the Ullswater, Angle Tarn and other hills surrounding Patterdale and Hartsop. This particular 'pilgrimage' started off as 'just another climb'. Yet this was to be perhaps the penultimate climb of my life. Why? Because in Thomas Merton's words this particular climb became symbolic of the *universal* spiritual journey of all those who climb the mountain of the Lord. All of this became clear only after that day's climb.

COMMITMENT AND PERSEVERANCE

The start

The climb to the crags starts at Brotherswater Lake and initially is a steep climb to a ridge which leads south-west to Hart Crag. Despite the early morning start and being 'fresh and strong' the initial climb is demanding with frequent stops for deep breathing to replenish the oxygen supply. Very much like the beginning of the spiritual journey where there are often starts and stops as one for example adjusts to the daily discipline of setting aside times for silent meditation. Just getting started on either journey is a challenge. But on the spiritual journey seeing the 'Lord's mountain' ahead is usually enough impetus to get us up to that initial ridge. This is the first stage in the spiritual journey which goes from the 'valley' to the 'mountain top'. The mountain stands for a place of *encounter with God*.

The ridge

After 40 minutes of the steep climb it was up and on to a fairly level ridge with a beautiful panoramic view of Deepdale Beck to the right and Dovedale Beck to the left. My heart was lifted up. The sun was shining and everything looked like smooth sailing. Just a matter of hiking a few easy miles to the base of Hart and Dove Crags. An ancient stone wall erected to contain sheep stretched forward on the ridge and gave me a sense of security, permanence and direction. There was just one small flicker of apprehension. Suddenly straight ahead the view of Hart and Dove Crags was shrouded in dense cloud and darkness. Not only cloud, as I was later to learn to my chagrin, but fog, rain and a severe wind.

But for now the path ahead looked comfortable and rather easy. Our spiritual pilgrimage, after the initial effort, also often leads along a straight and narrow path. We seem to glide along confident that we can attain our goal without too much trouble. God carries us along in his arms. All's right with the world. Self-denial, meditation all seem easy, effortless.

The fright

After an hour's walk along the ridge suddenly a fright, a moment of panic. In the distance about 30 hunting dogs, no doubt turned loose by their owner in the valley, seemed to be heading directly for me. As they came closer and closer my apprehension and fear increased dramatically. The idea of being torn apart by 30 fierce dogs in a remote area of Cumbria was not overly attractive. I prayed for deliverance. Physically my only hope of escape seemed to be to climb up on the stone wall. The dogs kept running directly at me but suddenly only a few yards away they veered to the left and each in turn jumped the wall and disappeared down the valley. So much for feeling safe on the wall.

What does this last experience have to do with the spiritual pilgrimage? It seems to me that to grow spiritually demands trust, to rely on God's plan and his power, not on our own strength. Perhaps the dogs are a reminder that we have to be prepared to come to grips with our shadow side and the beasts inside us. Climbing to the mountain is a stripping process, meant to purify us at ever deeper levels of selfishness and pride. This stripping lays bare our inner emptiness. This process (like the dogs) can be terrifying. God is asking us to make ourselves vulnerable and is asking for total trust in his capacity to lead us along the right path. He wants us to trust that he will take care of us, to have faith in his presence and power.

Up to the top

After a one and a half hour hike along the ridge towards 'the mountain' the weather started to deteriorate. The wind rose to gale strength. Finally at the base of Hart Crag a terrible moment of decision. Sitting down on some rocks to rest, I knew there was a terrible choice to be made. Should I turn back? The sun was shining back there where I had come from! Looking up an almost perpendicular gully of jagged rocks I could not even see the top of Hart Crag hidden in the dense cloud. I had no idea how far I had to go and this was perplexing. Humanly speaking the temptation was to turn back, to give up, perhaps to try another day. Then suddenly God's grace! It became abundantly clear to me that I had absolutely no choice but to go on . . . to climb the Crag. And with the decision to go on suddenly came the strength. The 45 minutes of upward climbing was surprisingly easy. Even the fierce wind abated in the gully leading to the top.

In the spiritual journey and in the daily practice of meditation there comes a time when we are tempted to turn back. It even happened with God's chosen people in the Sinai desert. As Charles Cummings points out in *Spirituality and the Desert Experience* God promised the Israelites 'that he would lead them through the desert to a land of freedom and plenty. But the Israelites vacillated back and forth between trusting God's promise and doubting it.' At one point the majority opted to go back to Egypt and slavery rather than put up with the trials and hardships of the desert. Only those who had faith, whose trust in God's presence and promise remained firm, were permitted to enter the promised land.

The journey to the mountain of the Lord is not a journey of consolation and surety. It is often a journey of doubt. Our spirit of trust in the Lord is put to the test. On our spiritual journey we have to trust that God is present and that he loves us even when he seems permanently absent. He is teaching us not to get discouraged if we have periods of meditation where he seems to have disappeared, where we are totally distracted. Again he is teaching us to trust in his travel plan... that he is leading us along the right path.

The top of Hart Crag

Finally at the top of Hart Crag a moment of exuberance and consolation at making it to the summit. But only a brief moment. No sunshine up here. A little bit of an eerie feeling. Again a dense cloud, rain, fog and a fierce wind. There is only a faint outline of a path. The whole idea now, humanly speaking, is survival, finding a path along the ridge of the Crags and then locating a path back home again. Lots of fear and anxiety up here. Am I heading along the right path? Am I all alone up here? What happens if I fall and injure myself? The sudden realisation that one could die up here. There is a lot of questioning up on the top. It soon becomes clear that there is going to be no rest at the top of this particular mountain. Not even a moment to sit down to eat and drink. It is now simply a question of seeking and searching for a path back home.

There is both beauty and harshness up here but not much opportunity to admire the beauty. Two hours are spent in frantic searching. It is hard work up here. In the midst of the fog and rain though I meet several fellow hikers who have climbed to the top of Hart Crag. We exchange pleasantries and directions. But no one seems able to tell me precisely how to get back to Brotherswater and my starting point on the journey. They have all taken different routes and are following their own paths.

In a spiritual sense being on top of the mountain demands even greater trust in God's continual, unseen presence and protection. We have to have a spirit of cheerful trust as our eyes look for the path ahead that leads to home. We also have to traverse the top of the mountain for as long as God wants us there. There is also a question of waiting on God. Waiting for him to show us the right path, waiting for deliverance. God does carry us along though. The mountain top transforms us, deepens, enriches and – divinises us.

It leads us to inner freedom, peace, love and joy. The more we accept the harshness of the mountain top, the more do we discover the depths of God's mercy. This is the time in our spiritual journey when we need great faith. It is also a time when we need the support and encouragement of others on the same pilgrimage. We need to know we are not alone.

Finally though, when all is said and done, I am lost on top of Hart Crag. I seem to be going around in circles, passing the same point twice. I have lost the faint outline of the path. Not only have I lost the path but for the last two hours there seems to be no fellow humans left up here. It is scary. Just fog, rain, cloud and the incessant noisy wind. I now have to admit I have absolutely no idea where the path to home is and I have no idea even how to get off the mountain. I have visions of staying up here all night and fears as to the danger in the wind, rain and increasing cold. There is a terrifying feeling of aloneness and helplessness. It is also getting darker. Yet I am praying fervently and continually for deliverance.

The way home

Then suddenly for some unaccountable reason I turn 45 degrees to my left off the vague path I was following and head directly for a side of the mountain shrouded in fog and cloud. There to my utter amazement and relief I see sunshine down in a valley and then discover the *one* and *only* path on the entire mountain leading down to my starting point and home. Amazement and sheer joy. The Lord has delivered me! After a half-hour climb down into the sunshine I finally sit down to eat and drink after the six hours of straight climbing. Another two hours and I am home at last for a hot bath and rest.

In retrospect

What can one learn from the experience? St Paul to the Corinthians comes to mind. 'My grace is sufficient for you, my power is made perfect in weakness' (2 Cor. 12:9). The mountain top seems to be a place of spiritual darkness and aridity where the only response is to be guided along the path by pure faith. We indeed learn that the only light to guide the steps of the spiritual mountaineer is a light burning in one's own heart, the light of faith. The mountain top is a transcendent experience that brings us to commitment. Commitment is the way of the mountain. We must continue to follow the path of our daily periods of meditation. And commitment is by definition death of self. It is finding life by losing life. The mountain top forces us to go beyond ourselves, transcend ourselves. The mountain top is where we go to seek the face of God. 'Lift up your eyes to the mountain' (Ps. 121:1).

In the deep darkness and spiritual aridity of the mountain top the God of light and love sustains and carries us along with his grace, stays with us and leads us along his *own* path. On the spiritual journey we begin to discover God's caring presence even in his apparent absence. The mountain top experience is the beginning of deep personal and spiritual growth. It is not the end of the journey but it does lead us on the path homeward. When we can no longer trust and rely on our own ability to make sense of the mountain experience, we learn the lesson of trusting in his constant care and guidance. At that point on the mountain when we feel most empty and deserted we discover that God has been leading us all along.

> Come let us climb the Lord's mountain
> that he may instruct us in his ways
> and we may walk in his paths.
> (Isa. 2:3–4)

19
The role of the Christian Meditation group

In contact with others we awaken to the deeper truth of our being that we are meant to see, and so we learn to travel beyond ourselves. This is why meditating regularly, whether daily or weekly, with the same group or community is such a source of healthy sustenance to our pilgrimage. We cannot maintain the delusion of an isolated pilgrimage when we are present with others. And yet, this very physical and spiritual presence recalls us to a deeper personal commitment to stillness, to silence and to fidelity.

The group or community similarly signals the end to all false heroism and self-dramatization. Being in touch with the ordinary failings and limitations of others puts our response and fidelity into the perspective which we need for balance and harmony in our life. In the presence of others we know ourselves . . .

Every day I am more amazed at the range and variety of people who really hear the message of the teaching about meditation, who hear it from some deep and perhaps unsuspected stillness within themselves. And I am even more inspired that so many remain faithful to the discipline and the fidelity that makes the hearing really significant. They are people of all ages and backgrounds, educational, social and religious. But they have all discovered a common centre, Christ, who lives in their hearts and in the heart of all creation.

(JOHN MAIN, *The Present Christ*)

The weekly group meeting

The special legacy of the life and teaching of John Main is the remarkable growth of small Christian Meditation groups meeting weekly in various countries of the world. It was John Main's hope that the teaching would be shared in an organic way through small groups of men and women meeting regularly in homes, parishes, schools and work-places.

He had a profound understanding of the ancient tradition of

THE ROLE OF THE CHRISTIAN MEDITATION GROUP 113

Christians gathering together to pray. As Laurence Freeman has pointed out, he saw this modern development of contemplation as originating in the communities of faith and the liturgy of the heart of the early Church. These early Christians also gathered in small groups in one another's houses. This coming together in prayer formed the 'koinonia' or the social interaction and communion that was the distinguishing mark and power of the early Church.

John Main had a clear understanding of the need of a community of faith that would solidify one's own commitment to the spiritual discipline of meditation while at the same time making the teaching available to newcomers. Our human experience tells us that meeting with others on a common pilgrimage can give us the support we need to carry on the journey. Experience has also demonstrated that when a group starts in a new geographic area, people who have never meditated before will join the group. *New* groups introduce *new* people to meditation.

There are a number of good reasons why we should meet in a meditation group once a week. Meeting in a group promotes a spiritual bond amongst the members and a mutual concern between those who have set out on a common pilgrimage. As mentioned the meditation group is really a community of faith much like the community of early Christians in St Paul's time. In commenting about meditating in a group, Father William Johnston SJ, in his book, *The Inner Eye of Love*, says: 'For example we can sit together in silent and wordless meditation. And in such a situation we can feel not only the silence in our hearts but the silence of the whole group. Sometimes such silence will be almost palpable and it can unite people more deeply than any words.'

The heart of the meditation group meeting is the sharing of silence together. This is the primary reason why people around the world are spontaneously starting small groups to meditate weekly together. The power and strength of meditating together comes from the words of Jesus, 'Where two or three are gathered in my name there I am in the midst of them' (Matt. 18:20). This is the primary reason for getting together once a week. It is as if meditators instinctively realise that this is a journey that is difficult to make alone; it is a journey that is so much easier if we make it with others. It is true that no one else can meditate for us, that we meditate in solitude each day, but at the same time we realise that we need the support of others if we are to persevere on this journey.

The group setting enables beginners to learn 'how' to meditate. Newcomers can be integrated into a group at any point in time. In addition the weekly group meeting provides support and encouragement to those who might be discouraged or experiencing difficulties 'on the path'. All of us need, from time to time, the encouragement of seeing others faithful and committed to the discipline.

We also need to absorb the teaching more deeply and we do so at the weekly meeting with the playing of a taped talk by John Main. There are now about 200 talks by Father John available on various aspects of meditation. These talks give instruction and deepen motivation and so help us to persevere on the path. They give us a spiritual boost each week: part of the food we need for the journey.

The question and answer period at the end of the meeting often helps immeasurably in clarifying situations not only for the questioner but also for other members of the group.

Groups meet in diverse locations and at various hours throughout the day and evening. There are now over 1,000 groups worldwide meeting in 35 countries in homes, apartments, schools, churches, rectories, religious communities, Christian Meditation centres, chapels, universities, prisons, government office buildings, a department store, senior citizens' homes and factories.

Lists of groups and times of meetings are available from Christian Meditation group leaders in various countries. An international list of groups is available from The International Centre, The World Community for Christian Meditation, 23 Kensington Sq., London W8 5HN.

Starting a group

Before starting a new group, one should be sure of one's personal commitment to the daily discipline of meditation. In practical terms this probably means about six months of daily meditation before starting a group.

There is a very helpful booklet available to help potential new group leaders. It is titled *The Christian Meditation Group: How to Start a Group, How to Lead a Group*. It covers such topics as where groups meet, the structure of a group meeting, how to communicate with others about the group, sample church bulletin announcements, and a variety of other topics relating to starting a new group. A copy of this booklet can be obtained through Medio Media, the World Community For Christian Meditation book/tape distribution outlets in various countries.

The booklet points out that people sometimes say 'I could never start a group because I could never give a talk, and what if there are questions I couldn't answer?' To pass on the teaching it is not necessary to give eloquent talks. The leader is not expected to be a guru or an expert on all the teaching. In fact a joke among one group of meditators is that 'the leader is the one who presses the "play" button on the tape recorder'. In many groups members take turns monthly in performing the function of the leader. The tapes of John Main are a precious resource to group leaders all over the world. They give a continuous and deepening teaching week by week. Gradually they bring each person who listens to them to find their own voice and way of communicating the teaching. Any questions at the end of the meeting are often answered by other members of the group, which shows how the Spirit teaches us in and through each other.

The fear of failure says Laurence Freeman, can stop us starting a group just as it can block us from doing many things . . . even meditating! Fear or a sense of failure is an egotistical idea and it is a sure sign that we are still trying to control events and people. But meditation groups, if they are schools of faith, are not controlled. They are led by the Spirit. Meditation itself takes us beyond the dualism of success and failure, and frees us to do many things we once thought were impossible, including leading a meditation group.

Small is beautiful

John Main was an admirer of E. F. Schumacher (1911–77), author of the world best seller *Small is Beautiful*, in which Schumacher outlines his philosophy on the advantages of 'smallness' over the impersonality of 'largeness' in all areas of contemporary life.

In the light of Schumacher's principles, John Main saw the advantages of small groups of meditators meeting weekly and offering *personal* affirmation and encouragement to each other on their spiritual pilgrimage. Like Schumacher he did not like the top/down model of the hierarchically organised structure. The top/down structure is feudal and dominantly masculine, while the open group is more balanced, nurturing and supportive.

Perhaps William James (1842–1910), author of *Varieties of Religious Experience*, has put this idea of smallness most succinctly:

> I am done with great things
> And big things, great institutions
> And big success, and I am for those
> Tiny invisible molecular moral
> Forces that work from individual
> To individual, creeping through
> The crannies of the world like
> So many rootlets, or like the

Capillary oozing of water,
Yet which, if you give them time, will
Rend the hardest monuments
Of man's pride.

A small meditation group is a spiritual cell and therefore it cannot be measured by materialistic standards. A group of 20 is not necessarily better or stronger than a group of 3. When it comes to this principle of 'smallness' numbers are quite unimportant.

20
Some other aspects of the journey

Meeting and meditating with so many who follow the extraordinary and wonderful pilgrimage in the usual course of their ordinary daily lives makes me see more clearly than ever before the true nature of this journey we are making together. We know it as a journey of faith, of expanding capacity to love and to be loved; and so also as an expanding vision of reality.

And we know it too as a way that demands more and more faith. Mountains get steeper the closer you approach the summit and the path narrows. But so also the view becomes vaster, more inspiring and more humbling, strengthening us for the deeper commitment required of us for the last stages of the climb . . .

Meditation, as the way of a life centred faithfully and with discipline on prayer, is our way into this true experience of spirit, of the Spirit. As anyone who follows this way soon comes to know for themselves, its demand upon us increases with each step we take along the pilgrimage. As our capacity to receive the revelation increases so too does the natural impulse we feel to make our response, our openness, more generous, more unpossessive.

The strange and wonderful thing is that this demand is unlike any other demand made upon us. Most demands upon us seem to limit our freedom, but this demand is nothing less than an invitation to enter into full liberty of spirit – the liberty we enjoy when we are turned away from self. What seems the demand for absolute surrender is in fact the opportunity for the infinite realization of our potential. But to understand this we cannot flinch from the fact that the demand is absolute and consequently so must our response be.

(JOHN MAIN, *The Present Christ*)

Our image of God

In all probability our image of God affects our meditation practice. There can be a problem for newcomers to meditation in coming to an understanding of this 'inner Christ', of a God who lives at the centre of our being.

In a recent issue of the *New Yorker* magazine there is a cartoon of a heavenly office with a very elaborate closed door marked 'God'. A secretary with wings sits outside the office. Along comes a worried man, sheaves of paper in his hands, who says to the secretary 'Is he the God of the Old or New Testament this morning?' Unfortunately many of us have been conditioned from early childhood to have a warped Old Testament image of God. We think of God as being a harsh judge of our frailty or as being distant from ourselves. He is the God of Genesis, a Sistine Chapel God who sits somewhere out there and creates the world. The problem with this image of God is that He seems far away and distant. This image portrays a God outside of us. The New Testament image of God in St John's gospel tells us that in fact he is just the opposite, that he is the deepest source within us, an inner presence that is closer to us and deeper within ourselves than our own conscious self.

Thomas Merton points out that for many people God is a sphinx-like and arbitrary force bearing down upon us with implacable hostility, leading us to lose faith in a God we cannot find it possible to love.

For some people God is a God of retribution, a policeman, a bogeyman. But this is not a New Testament image of God. On the contrary, Jesus gives us the real image of His Father in the story of the prodigal son. The prodigal son leaves his father and sins in the big city. When he returns the father does not criticise him, judge him, is not even angry with him. In fact, it is just the opposite. The father embraces the son, declares a holiday, and kills the fatted calf for a big celebration. This is the New Testament image of God. God loves us, embraces us, can hardly wait to welcome us back when we have strayed. This is the God who says 'behold I stand at the door and knock; if anyone hears my voice and opens the door, I will come and eat with them and they with me'. (Rev. 3:20).

St John's gospel is all about a God who lives within us. In meditation we are concerned with the inner Jesus who dwells in our hearts. This is the Jesus who lives within us and tells us, 'in that day you will know that I live in the Father, and you live in me, and I in you' (John 14:20). Meditation is this inner journey to find God within. But in reality we do not have to seek God's presence. He is already within us. He has already found us. We must simply experience and realize this truth through the spiritual discipline of our daily periods of meditation.

This is the inner Christ in St John's gospel who says: 'make your home in me, as I make mine in you. If anyone loves me they will keep my word, and my Father will love them and we shall come to them and make our home with them' (John 14:23). 'I am the

SOME OTHER ASPECTS OF THE JOURNEY 119

vine, you are the branches. Whoever remains in me, bears fruit in plenty' (John 15:5). 'God is love and anyone who lives in love lives in God and God lives in them' (1 John 4:16). This *living within* is beautifully acknowledged by St Paul in his letter to the Ephesians 3:16–19.

> Out of his infinite glory, may he give you the power through his Spirit for your hidden self to grow strong, so that Christ may live in your hearts through faith, and then, planted in love and built on love, you will with all the saints have the strength to grasp the breadth and the length, the height and the depth; until knowing the love of Christ, which is beyond all knowledge, you are filled with the utter fullness of God.

In the writings of St John and St Paul we discover the risen Christ of the New Testament who lives *within* us.

Sharing the teaching

John Main once said that if we are faithful to the daily recitation of our mantra, we cannot help but want to share this gift of meditation with others. Gifts are meant to be given away. Jesus says 'freely have you received, freely give' (Matt 10:8).

The question is: How do we share this gift with others? For many of us it will simply be open to responding to questions about Christian Meditation from family, friends and work associates. It is important here not to be too forceful but simply to be factual and objective about the teaching and the practice.

Perhaps it is a question of using whatever talents we have in order to make it known that our particular meditation group exists and is open to new members. For some of us this may simply be communicating this information by word of mouth to neighbours, parishioners, contacts. For others it may be placing a small notice in a church bulletin or asking a parish priest or minister to make a pulpit announcement. Perhaps it means someone putting a simple typed announcement about a meditation group on a notice-board in a shop or at work. Some people may have the talent to write an article for the weekly secular or religious newspaper in their community. Some people may feel confident enough to volunteer to give a talk about meditation to parish organisations or other groups. The principle is 'to each according to his or her talents and abilities'.

There are some people who may object to this type of market-place communications. Perhaps they are waiting for that voice booming out of the heavens announcing the formation of a new meditation group. But God does not usually work that way. He usually works through the creativity and instrumentality of human beings. In other words, he uses our God-given talents to do his work.

Of course our message should be *honest, simple, factual* with *no promises* and in *good taste*. But having said that why should we be shy of using every method of communication that reaches the public today? If St Paul were alive today, he would not be writing with a quill pen; he would probably be using a word processor and E-mail. Let us not be afraid of using the communication tools available to us.

There is also the important role for many of us of actually starting a meditation group either in our own homes or in some institutional location. It is by starting meditation groups in new areas of a city, suburbs or small town that we can really share this gift of meditation with others. Experience has shown that when a new meditation group starts, people who have never meditated before will join that group.

Of course, to leave an established group to start a new group requires *courage*. We do get used to an established pattern and we do develop friends within the original group. We hate to leave an old group. But how are we ever going to share this gift of meditation unless some of us launch out into the deep and establish new groups?

Again we have been given a gift. But gifts are to share . . . to give away. We are all pilgrims on the way, and as meditators the one God-given gift we can share with others is to hand on the teaching of Christian Meditation to others in one form or another.

The prayerful reading of Scripture

John Main felt that the teaching of silence and stillness in prayer was firmly rooted in both the Old and New Testaments. (See Chapter 6.) He also felt strongly that the prayerful reading of Scripture was an ideal preparation for the silence of meditation.

In the monastic tradition *lectio divina* or the reflective reading, listening to and digesting of Scripture was seen as an integral part of the monk's spiritual development. *Lectio divina* was meant to lead a monk from the written word to *resting* in the Lord. In other words this monastic tradition of *lectio divina* was meant to be the door that opened a monk to the contemplative experience. To some extent this tradition has been lost in monastic communities. That is why John Main felt a return to the prayerful reading of Scripture was a necessary complement to the mantra in preparation for bringing one to the interior silence of meditation.

The role of a teacher

Meditation as taught in the various religions, is traditionally handed down through a holy and learned teacher. In Christianity it was an early practice for young travelling monks to seek out a holy father (*abba*) who would unfold to them 'the prayer of the heart'. John Cassian and his monk companion Germanus, for instance, sought out the holy man Abba Isaac and asked Isaac to teach them to pray.

Of course for the Christian it is the indwelling risen Jesus who is the living teacher: 'Once Jesus was in a certain place praying, and when he ceased, one of his disciples said to him "Lord, teach us to pray as John taught his disciples" ' (Luke 11:1). Meeting with a teacher can be the essential encounter of our spiritual lifetime. Many meditators have recognised John Main as their teacher after hearing only a few brief words from one of his talks or reading a brief passage from one of his books. The finding of a teacher can be the decisive turning point in one's life. John Main exemplifies the true teacher who is a transparent medium through which the Spirit of Christ is perceived.

To learn any skill or discipline one needs a teacher. A teacher not only indicates the way, but offers discernment, encouragement and assists the student to avoid any pitfalls. In the case of meditation it is the teacher who traditionally introduces one to the discipline of the mantra.

Those who practice Christian Meditation look to the Spirit first as the teacher with the help of John Main. For those experiencing problems on the path of meditation help is available from spiritual friends worldwide who share John Main's teaching on this tradition. Assistance with any difficulties is also available within the weekly meditation group meetings from other members of the group who often have faced the same experiences.

Spiritual guidance and the soul friend

A question often asked is whether one requires a spiritual director/guide on the path of Christian Meditation. One must distinguish here between, on the one hand, a teacher of prayer such as John Main, and on the other hand, those who offer guidance and discernment on one's personal spiritual journey.

In regard to the teaching of Christian Meditation we have an incomparable resource in the 200 cassette-taped talks by John Main and his many books. In addition meditators receive guidance and nourishment for the practice of meditation through Christian Meditation retreats, conferences, audio/video tapes, books, the quarterly Christian Meditation newsletter, and from weekly meetings of Christian Meditation groups. The real teacher, of course, is the *Spirit*.

However, the art and practice of spiritual guidance goes beyond the teaching of Christian Meditation. It is an ancient practice in Christianity. In the wisdom and sayings of the fourth-century desert fathers/mothers handed down to us, we see holy and wise monks constantly giving personal spiritual advice and guidance to younger monks. In the Middle Ages it was St Bernard of Clairvaux who said 'the one who directs himself is a fool'.

However one must point out here that there are great changes in the twentieth century from the times of the desert fathers and St Bernard of Clairvaux. For one thing we have a wide range of *books*, spiritual classics, studies on the psychological understanding of the spiritual journey as well as treatises on spiritual development and growth. For those interested specifically in spiritual direction, one of the most comprehensive contemporary books is *The Art of Spiritual Guidance* by Carolyn Gratton.

In her book she points out that a holy and wise spiritual guide can offer discernment on trying to find God's will in regard to a decision to be made, as well as assist people through transitional periods in their spiritual development. A spiritual guide can also assist one to maintain a balance between spiritual and external activities. However, in these days of the Church's increasing appreciation of human freedom, Gratton maintains that few even of the most traditional contemporary guides would advise persons who come for direction to 'give themselves over' or 'give up their own will' in blind obedience to the guidance of anyone but the Holy Spirit.

Self-deception as well as psychological problems are at time possible on the spiritual journey. At times we could need the prudence and loving care of a holy spiritual guide, one who can recognise the movements of the Spirit in our spiritual life. For those who are meditating it is important that this spiritual guide understands and has had experience with the teaching and practice of Christian Meditation. In the sixteenth century St John of the Cross lamented the incompetence of many spiritual directors who hinder rather than help people along the contemplative path. It is a truism that only a contemplative can offer contemplative guidance for others. St Teresa of Avila also found it frustrating dealing with so many incapable spiritual guides over a 20 year period. She wrote of this

SOME OTHER ASPECTS OF THE JOURNEY

period, 'Through them I suffered so much that I now wonder how I could endure it'.

What is needed for the meditator is support and encouragement to persevere on this journey of prayer. A guide who can offer friendship and support can be of great help when one is going through a dry, difficult time in meditation when God seems absent from our pilgrimage.

Of course we must never forget that the great spiritual master and guide lives within our own heart. Our first priority is to listen to the Spirit. Having stated this, what do we look for in a human guide and where do we find such people? Again we must also keep in mind that an inexperienced guide or a person not in touch with the contemplative tradition and the practice of Christian Meditation could thwart one's spiritual growth.

It would seem that we do not have a plethora of holy, experienced and contemplative spiritual guides for the many contemporary meditators on the inner spiritual pilgrimage. It has been said 'If God wanted each meditator to have a spiritual director, they (spiritual guides) would be hanging on trees like apples, ripe for picking'. Unfortunately there is not much picking these days! The universal complaint is 'Where can I find a good spiritual guide?'

Perhaps at this point we should change the terminology. Kenneth Leech in his book *Soul Friend*, suggests the Irish Celtic tradition has something to teach us.

> It was seen (in Ireland) as necessary for everyone to possess a soul-friend, and the saying, 'Anyone without a soul-friend is a body without a head' (attributed both to Brigit and to Comgall) became an established Celtic proverb ... the soul-friend was essentially a counsellor and guide, and the office was not seen in specifically sacramental terms. Often the soul-friend was a layman or laywoman.

Leech points out that spiritual guidance involves more than answers to problems and ready made remedies. He says a soul-friend is a person of humility and gentleness who recognises our own uniqueness and listens with caring love to the movements of the Spirit within us. What is needed with a soul-friend is a rapport, a union of minds and hearts. Soul-friends will know each other at a deeper level of awareness.

Perhaps we have been looking for spiritual guides in the wrong places. As pointed out, the best spiritual guide resides in our own heart. However, if we feel the need for additional guidance on the spiritual journey perhaps a soul-friend is the answer. That soul-friend you may already know. It may be a member of your meditation group. It will be a person with openness of heart; a person who understand the need for silence and stillness in your life. It may well be a person who walks along the road to Emmaus with you, and sets your heart on fire. That soul-friend could be a fellow human being or it may also be the Spirit that you have already found in your meditative practice in your own heart.

Smashing the mirror of the ego: leaving self behind

In commonday language, the essence of meditation is to leave the ego behind. We are not trying to see with the ego what is happening. Ego-vision is limited by its own self-centredness. The eye with which we see without limit is the eye that cannot see itself. The paradox of meditation is that once we give up trying to see and to possess, then we see all and all things are ours.

(JOHN MAIN, *Word Made Flesh*)

The problems of the ego begin with terminology, depending on which psychological tradition you follow. However to simplify definitions the word ego comes from the Latin for 'I'. It is what gives us our individual uniqueness and our identity. Our true self is made in the image of God in which every human being is created. The ego is a mirror-image of the true self.

Unfortunately in all of us this mirror image can be mistaken for reality and become a false self that develops in *our* likeness rather than in the likeness of God. This is where we get the term 'egocentric'. Many spiritual teachers, including John Main, simply equate this false self with the term 'ego' or 'egoism'. But we must always remember that our ego in the initial stages of our life gives us our uniqueness and identity. It is not bad in itself – but it can become a point of illusion, self-seeking and self-aggrandisement.

The false self develops many masks to hide the true self. Our false self always wants to be at centre stage. The false self wants to be served first and think of itself first. Others come second. Our false self believes the world revolves around *me*. It is always seeking control, power, adulation. The false self wants to control every situation and manipulate others.

John Main speaks about our false self and the need of 'smashing the mirror' of our ego. He says that when we are united to God 'as our supreme power source' we break through the mirror of the 'hyper-self-consciousness of egoism'. According to John Main the root of 'sin' is this self-consciousness which is a mirror, as it were, between God and our self, reflecting only our image and not God's image which is our true identity. This mirror must be smashed says Father John and meditation is the means of smashing it. But this smashing however is non-violent; it is the work of love. There is

SOME OTHER ASPECTS OF THE JOURNEY 125

absolutely no doubt that on the spiritual path one must struggle for this detachment from egoism and self-will.

The Buddha in commenting on the ego said 'For those whom ego overcomes, sufferings spread like wild grass'. The ego's drive for self-aggrandisement inevitably leads it away from God.

William Law (1686–1761) the English Anglican mystic put it this way in *Christian Regeneration*: 'See here the whole truth in short. All sin, all death, damnation and hell is nothing else but this kingdom of self, or the various operations of self love, self-esteem, and self-seeing which separate the soul from God.'

Swami Abhishiktananda (Henri Le Saux) in *The Man and His Teachings* says:

> The fundamental step in salvation, or conversion, is taken at the level of the human heart, that is to say, at the deepest centre of our being. This conversion, this metanoia of the Gospel, is the abandoning of all self-centredness, of all egoism; it is a total turning back of the whole being to God. In other words it is to place oneself in the presence of the Saviour.

And again he is quoted in the same book as saying:

> Jesus himself taught that a person has to abandon everything, to put everything at risk, if they are to enter the kingdom. The Gospel is essentially a renunciation of and an uprooting of the self, of the ego, leaving it behind and following in the footsteps of the Master.

The false self exists, but at the level of illusion. It has no ultimate reality. But we can all choose to drop the mask, the illusion of this false self and achieve our true identity in God. The journey to our true self *is* the journey of meditation because in the deep silence of our meditation we acknowledge our dependence on Jesus. Thomas Merton says God possesses the secret of my identity, and the only way to find this true identity is by losing the false self in him.

In meditation our 'egoism' or false self melts slowly away as the focus of attention shifts from self to God and then to others. Why does this happen? Because the saying of the mantra is an act of pure *selflessness*. Each time we say the mantra we renounce and leave behind 'my' *own* thoughts, 'my' *own* words, 'my' *own* concerns, 'my' *own* fears, 'my' *own* anxieties. In losing these selfish possessions we begin to lose the false self. In this detachment which meditation requires, the mask, the phoney disguise, is stripped away to reveal where the true *I* has been hiding. Like a moth our false self is drawn to the flame where it must die. It must be discarded, says Thomas Merton, like an old snake skin.

Meditation develops a spirit of forgiveness. Many spiritual writers point out that forgiveness is one of the primary ways to combat the ego. When we forgive others for insults, real or imagined, we undercut the emotional resentment of the ego. As author Ken Wilber has pointed out in his book *Grace and Grit*, the fundamental mood of the ego is never to forgive, never to forget. Forgiveness undermines the very existence of the ego. (See this chapter on 'The Need to Forgive'.)

The *Course of Miracles* puts it this way:

> What could you want forgiveness cannot give? Do you want peace? Forgiveness offers it. Do you want happiness, a quiet mind, a certainty of purpose, and a sense of worth and beauty that transcends the world? Do you want care and safety, and the warmth of sure protection always? Do you want a quietness that cannot be disturbed, a gentleness that never can be hurt, a deep abiding comfort, and a rest so perfect it can never be upset?
>
> All this forgiveness offers you and more.
> Forgiveness offers everything I want.
> Today I have accepted this as true.
> Today I have received the gifts of God.

Meditation helps us to shed the false self because in fact it is about self-forgetfulness. As John Main says, it is about taking the searchlight off ourselves, it is about self-transcendence. Could this be what Jesus meant when he said, 'if anyone wishes to follow me, they must leave *self* behind, take up their cross daily and follow me' (Matt. 16:24)?

The Chinese poet Li Po put it this way:

> We meditate together, the mountain and me
> Until only the mountain remains.

There is the story about a sculptor who carved a superb statue of an elephant. When asked how he had done it, he replied he had started with a block of granite and then simply chipped away at everything that was *not* the elephant. That is the work of meditation. Chipping away at our false self, so that our true self, the image and likeness of God may appear. Gradually we are purified in meditation of this false self and discover that God is within us and that he is the ground of our being.

Of course the journey from the false self to the true self is not always a pleasant, easy journey. There are hiccups along the way. We do not like to change and God who is love transforms us. To change is to die. It has very much to do with the passage from St John's gospel, 'truly I say to you, unless a grain of wheat falls into the earth and dies, it remains alone, *but if it dies it bears much fruit'* (John 12:24).

In meditation something dies within us, our false self, but something new is born. In starting off on this path we cling to what is familiar and dread the journey to what is unfamiliar. That is why Father John says meditation at times requires courage and in the final analysis is a path of pure faith.

On the path of meditation our true self is more and more revealed and the shadow of the false self slowly dissolves. In meditation the mask of the false self is peeled from our face and we find ourselves totally humbled and dependent on God. As Thomas Merton says, the false self is the 'smoke self' and will disappear like smoke up a chimney.

Through the discipline of daily meditation our true self is slowly revealed. When this happens we can cry out with St Paul 'it is no longer *I* that lives, but Christ lives in me' (Gal. 2:20). Now the spiritual journey seriously begins. Now having found our true self we can begin to really love. We have found our true identity in love and our true self in selflessness.

Keep death before one's eyes

In *Death the Inner Journey,* the last talk given by John Main in Montreal only a few months before his own death, he pointed out that not only must we all die but we must learn how to die well.

Father Laurence Freeman in the Preface to *Death the Inner Journey,* points out,

> Being with John Main in his own last days was to lose one's fear of death and to gain a sense of awe and reverence in its presence. Father John was the most lively and life-loving of human beings. He never lost his sense of humor or sense of wonder at the mystery of life through all of his final sufferings. But even in the best of health he was always clearly conscious of the shortness of time and he was as ready to die the next day as in ten years. This realism of death was rooted in the joy of the reality of God that he discovered in meditation.

According to Father Laurence, John Main taught with his life as well as by his dying and that is why his teaching lives.

Perhaps another way to answer this question is to quote a number of points made by Father John in *Death the Inner Journey* about meditation as a preparation for death.

- Meditation is well called *the first death*. Meditation is also

the essential preparation for the second death which is our definitive entry into eternal life.
- To live fully we must live in relationship with others. We must live our lives with love. To learn to love we must learn to die to self.
- Meditation is a way of dying *and* a way of living. While you are saying the mantra you are dying to what is the most difficult thing in the world for us to die to. We die to our own egoism, to our own self-centredness as we go beyond our own self-consciousness.
- The only way to prepare for death is to die day by day. This is the spiritual journey.
- Over the years we have been teaching meditation in this tradition we have known people who have started to meditate as they faced death and saw the horizon of their life approaching. Their attitude to death was transformed as they began to die to self day by day, as their preparation for the death of the body. It has been an inspiration and a revelation to us to see their growth in faith and hope as they learned to meditate even at this last stage of life.
- Both in the experience of love and of death we discover the reality of losing self. The wonder of each is to discover that we can lose self. In fact, we discover that the very reason for our creation is that we do lose self. And this is exactly what our meditation teaches us so well. To lose self, we must stop thinking about ourselves. We must place our centre outside of ourselves, beyond ourselves in another, in the Other.
- Within this vision we see life as preparation for death and we see death as preparation for life. If we are to meet our own death with hope it must be a hope built not on theory or on belief alone but on experience. We must know from experience that *death is an event in life*, an essential part of any life which is a perpetually expanding and self-transcending mystery. It seems to me that only the experience of the continuous death of the ego can lead us into this hope, lead us into an ever-deepening contact with the power of life itself. Only our own death to self-centredness can really persuade us of Death as the connecting link in the chain of perpetual expansion, the way to fullness of life.

The need to forgive

The words of Jesus are quite explicit about the need in our lives for reconciliation and forgiveness. In Matthew 5:23 he says 'If, when you are bringing your gift to the altar, you suddenly remember that your brother has a grievance against you, leave your gift where it is before the altar. First go and make your peace with your brother and only then come back and offer your gift.' And in Mark 11:25, Jesus says 'Whenever you stand praying, forgive, if you have anything against anyone'.

In the light of these words of Jesus it would be difficult to bring the gift of our self to meditation if we do not first forgive the wrongs of others and seek reconciliation with those we have offended or who have offended us.

In the beautiful story of the Prodigal Son, Jesus shows us what real forgiveness is all about. The Prodigal Son takes and spends his inheritance on riotous living in the big city and then returns home in humiliation and shame. The father (who is the New Testament image of our Heavenly Father) could retaliate, be angry, strip his son of any privileges or even send him away from the family home. But it is exactly the opposite. As he sees him coming in the distance, the father rushes out to welcome his son, embraces him and then calls a holiday and orders the family's treasured fatted calf to be killed for a big celebration. Talk about forgiveness!

We must also forgive others in our practice of meditation and this is a challenge for everyone. Again the words of Jesus leave no doubt how essential this teaching is. 'Then Peter came up and asked him, "Lord how often am I to forgive my brother if he goes on wronging me? As many as seven times?" Jesus replied, "I do not say seven times; I say seventy times seven" ' (Matt. 18–21).

If we want to grow spiritually on the path of meditation we have no choice but to forgive others, to wipe the slate clean, to start anew our relationships with those we have offended or who have offended us.

Humility and gratitude

A question one might ask is whether we have to worry about the problem of 'elitism' in Christian Meditation, feeling we have found the pearl of great price and others are still searching?

In every spiritual tradition and practice there is always a temptation to feel we have our act together, we are better, we are more advanced, this is the *only* way and many other variations on the theme. This is an insidious temptation because in fact in meditation, as John Main points out, we are all beginners as we return each day to our daily spiritual discipline. However, there is usually one saving grace for meditators. The practice of meditation is such a humbling and oftentimes difficult experience, that it is almost impossible to feel puffed up in regard to others on different spiritual paths.

Needless to say meditation is not the *only* spiritual path or the *only* way to pray. (This is also discussed in Chapter 14.) It behoves all those on the journey of meditation to be aware that it is a gratuitous call, to remain humble and thankful for the gift, and not to make comparisons with others who have been called by God to different spiritual paths.

The human consciousness of Christ

In *The Heart of Creation* John Main explains what he means by the 'human consciousness of Christ' and its relation to meditation:

> Meditation also teaches us that we can reach God the Father, through the human consciousness of Jesus, the Son, because we discover by meditating in faith that Jesus is the bridge that takes us to the further shore. He is the ferry that takes us across the river of egoism and launches us into the mainstream of divine love.
>
> Gradually, we come to realise that love is the basis of all reality, and that we are invited to live fully in his love through our commitment to gentleness, to compassion, to understanding. The great fact of the experience of meditating is that, once we do enter into the human consciousness of Jesus, we begin to see as he sees, to love as he loves, to understand as he understands, and to forgive as he forgives.

And again, from one of his talks:

> The way for each of us to God is through Jesus. The human consciousness of Jesus in his lifetime gradually became more open to the Father. The extraordinary effect of the Redemption is that now, in the glorified life of Jesus, his human consciousness is fully open to the Father. This human consciousness of Jesus is to be found in our own hearts. That's what the Indwelling of the Holy Spirit means. The supreme task of our life is to open our human consciousness to the human consciousness of Jesus...

In a recent conversation Father Laurence Freeman, John Main's spiritual heir, further elaborates upon this concept of 'the human consciousness of Christ':

SOME OTHER ASPECTS OF THE JOURNEY

John Main's particular contribution to the modern understanding of Christian meditation is his emphasis on the role of the human consciousness of Christ in our experience of God. Jesus in his fully human existence has completed the human journey by going beyond himself and finding himself anew in the Father. Even in his lifetime Jesus knew the Father as the origin of his being and the goal of his life. In his death and resurrection he uniquely discovered himself as the only-begotten Son. This journey of self-transcendence and self-discovery is the prayer of Jesus. As John Main says the essential prayer of the Christian is our entry into and union with the prayer of Jesus. This prayer is not limited by time or space. Jesus in his glorified humanity does not cease to be human. His relationship to us now is in his humanity – the universal compassion of his love spread universally through the Holy Spirit.

In meditation we open our human consciousness – with all its limitations and faults – to his human consciousness, unlimited and glorified in the divine life. Thus his consciousness (his body, mind and spirit) leads us to the fullness of being, to God, which he said was the purpose of his mission: 'I have come that you may have life, life in all its fullness'.

In meditating as Christians this is our understanding of what we are doing, why we are doing it and what happens as a result of doing it. Of course, in the meditation period itself we are not thinking of this but we are opening ourselves most deeply to its reality and our whole being (body, mind and spirit) will manifest the results of this experience in time.

21
The role of the World Community for Christian Meditation

The Community

The World Community was formed by the participants at the John Main Seminar in New Harmony, Indiana, USA in 1991 and is legally registered as a charity in their name in the United Kingdom. It is the spiritual steward of John Main's teaching.

The objective

The mission of the Community is *to communicate and nurture meditation as passed on through the teaching of John Main in the Christian tradition, in the spirit of serving the unity of all*. This is primarily realised through more than a thousand local meditation groups meeting in homes, religious institutions, colleges, hospitals, prisons and other venues in over 50 countries. In addition, 30 Christian Meditation Centres in different countries participate and contribute to this Community each in their own way. The coherence of the Community is rooted in the teaching of John Main and this creates a bond for dialogue and meditation with other faiths and traditions. A wide variety of expression and new forms of community are encouraged. The link with the monastic tradition, particularly the Benedictine, is highly valued.

The guiding board

The activities of the Community are overseen by a Guiding Board of eleven members, including the Director of the community and spiritual heir of John Main, Father Laurence Freeman, a Benedictine monk of Christ the King Monastery in London. The current (1996) chairperson of the Guiding Board is Robert Kiely, professor at Harvard University in Cambridge, Mass. Other members of the Board are from Canada, Australia, India, Singapore, the United Kingdom and the United States.

THE WORLD COMMUNITY FOR CHRISTIAN MEDITATION

The International Centre

The Community is served by an International Centre located in London. Under the direction of the Guiding Board, the International Centre performs the following vital functions:

- Cooperation and liaison with national, regional and local groups in pursuing the Community's world mission and objectives. An especially important task is supporting the teaching in economically disadvantaged countries and taking the teaching to areas where no groups or centres exist.
- Assistance to the Director in all his activities, including scheduling and planning for conferences, retreats and talks.
- Administrative and financial support services to the Community, including communications, media relations, preparation of resource materials, distribution of the Newsletter (outside North America), production of an International Directory of Christian Meditation groups and fund raising.
- Coordination/supervision for the planning and organisation of the annual John Main Seminar (which was led by the Dalai Lama in 1994, William Johnston in 1993, Jean Vanier in 1992 and Bede Griffiths in 1991).
- Administrative support to the Guiding Board and to Medio Media, the Community's publishing company.

The headquarters of the World Community for Christian Meditation is located at 23 Kensington Sq., London W8 5HN, England. Phone 0171-937-4679. Fax 0171-937-6790.

Epilogue

As one comes to the end of this book one is reminded of Hamlet's famous response to Polonius: 'WORDS, WORDS, WORDS.' There is a story which supplements Hamlet's famous dirge. It is about two monks, an old monk and a younger one. They were walking side by side along the bank of a river. The younger monk was asking the old monk all sorts of questions about the river. Where did it come from? Where was it going? How deep was it? How cold was it? How fast was it flowing? Questions, questions, questions. Then the old monk finally lost his patience. He turned and pushed the younger monk into the river. As he helped the younger monk climb out of the river, the old monk said 'now that you have all the answers, stop asking me those silly questions'.

After all the questions and answers and many words the key to Christian Meditation now is to jump in and get wet. There is only so much we can say *about* meditation. At some point we must enter into the experience itself, that stream of God's love, the Spirit of Christ within us. As John Main would say, the only important thing about meditation is to 'do it'.

Paul Harris

Bibliography and sources cited

Anonymous, *The Cloud of Unknowing*, (Introduction by William Johnston) Doubleday, 1973.
Augustine Baker, *Holy Wisdom*, Burns and Oates, 1964.
New Catholic Encyclopedia Vol 15, McGraw-Hill, article on John Cassian, 1967.
John Cassian, *Conferences*, Paulist Press, 1985.
Catechism of the Catholic Church, Geoffrey Chapman, 1994.
Edmund Colledge and James Walsh, *Julian of Norwich: Showings*, Paulist Press, 1978.
A Course in Miracles, Foundation for Inner Peace, 1992.
Deborah and George Cowley, *One Woman's Journey*, Novalis, 1992.
Charles Cummings, *Spirituality and the Desert Experience*, Dimension, 1978.
Odette Baumer-Despeigne, *The Spiritual Journey of Henry Le Saux – Abhishiktananda*, Cistercian Studies, No. 4, 1983.
Louis Dupré and James A. Wiseman, *Light from Light: An Anthology of Christian Mysticism*, Paulist Press, 1988.
Patrick Eastman, *Once a Mother, Always a Mother*, Monos Journal, May 1993.
Eknath Easwaran, *Meditation, Commonsense Directions for an Uncommon Life*, Nilgiri Press, 1978.
Eknath Easwaran, *The Unstruck Bell*, Nilgiri Press, 1993.
Meister Eckhart, *The Essential Sermons, Commentaries, Treatises and Defense*, Paulist Press and SPCK, 1981.
Laurence Freeman, *A Short Span of Days*, Novalis, 1991.
Laurence Freeman and Paul Harris, *The Christian Meditation Group: How to Lead a Group, How to Start a Group*, World Community for Christian Meditation, 1992.
R. M. French (trans.), *The Way of the Pilgrim*, Seabury Press, 1970.
François Gerard, *Going on a Journey*, privately printed, 1991.
Joseph Goldstein, *Insight Meditation, the Practice of Freedom*, Shambhala, 1993.
Carolyn Gratton, *The Art of Spiritual Guidance*, Crossroad, 1993.
Gregory of Nyssa, *The Life of Moses*, Paulist Press/SPCK, 1978.
Bede Griffiths, 'Discovering the Feminine' (video), More Than Illusion Films, 1993.

BIBLIOGRAPHY

Bede Griffiths, *The New Creation in Christ*, Darton, Longman and Todd, 1992.
Bede Griffiths, *The Golden String*, Collins Fount, 1979.
Bede Griffiths, *The Interface Between Christianity and Other Faiths*, (lecture), 1990.
Bede Griffiths, *The Marriage of East and West*, Collins Fount, 1983.
Paul Harris, *The Fire of Silence and Stillness: An Anthology of Quotations for the Spiritual Journey*, Darton, Longman and Todd, 1995.
Paul Harris, *John Main by Those Who Knew Him*, Darton, Longman and Todd/Novalis, 1991.
John J. Higgins, *Thomas Merton on Prayer*, Doubleday, 1973.
William James, *Varieties of Religious Experience*, The Modern Library, 1929.
John of the Cross, *The Collected Works of John of the Cross*, (Kavanaugh and Rodroguez (eds.), Institute of Carmelite Studies, 1974.
William Johnston, *Being in Love*, Collins, 1988.
William Johnston, *The Inner Eye of Love*, Collins Fount, 1981.
William Johnston, *The Mysticism of the Cloud of Unknowing*, Anthony Clarke Books and Abbey Press, 1975.
William Johnston, *Silent Music*, Fontana, 1976.
Thomas Keating, *Intimacy With God*, Crossroad, 1994.
Søren Kierkegaard, *The Sickness Unto Death*, Princeton University Press, 1954.
William Law, *The Life of Christian Devotion*, Abingdon Press, 1961.
William Law, *The Spirit of Love*, Classics of Western Spirituality, Paulist Press, 1978.
Kenneth Leech, *Soul Friend: A Study of Spirituality*, Darton, Longman and Todd, 1974.
André Louf, *Teach Us to Pray*, Darton, Longman and Todd, new edition, 1991.
Neil McKenty, *In the Stillness Dancing*, Darton, Longman and Todd, 1986.
John Main, *Christian Meditation: The Gethsemani Talks*. World Community for Christian Meditation, 1977.
John Main, *Community of Love*, Darton, Longman and Todd, 1990.
John Main, 'Death the Inner Journey' in *Community of Love*.
John Main, *The Heart of Creation*, Darton, Longman and Todd, 1988.
John Main, *The Inner Christ*, Darton, Longman and Todd, 1987.
John Main, *Letters From the Heart*, Crossroad, 1982.
John Main, 'The Other-Centredness of Mary' in *Community of Love*.
John Main, *Moment of Christ*, Darton, Longman and Todd, 1984.
John Main, *The Present Christ*, Darton, Longman and Todd, 1985.
John Main, *Word into Silence*, Darton, Longman and Todd, 1980.
John Main, *The Way of Unknowing*, Darton, Longman and Todd, 1989.

BIBLIOGRAPHY

Vandana Mataji, *Swami Abhishiktananda: The Man and His Teaching*, SPCK, 1986.
Thomas Merton, *The Inner Experience*, Cistercian Studies, 1983–84.
Thomas Merton, *Mystics and Zen Masters*, Dell, 1969.
Thomas Merton, *New Seeds of Contemplation*, New Directions, 1962.
Thomas Merton, *The Tears of the Blind Lions*, New Directions, 1949.
Thomas Merton, *The Waters of Siloe*, Harcourt Brace, 1949.
Thomas Merton, *The Way of Chuang Tzu*, New Directions, 1965.
Thomas Merton, *What is Contemplation*, Templegate, 1950.
Thomas Merton, *The Wisdom of the Desert*, New Directions, 1961.
New Yorker Magazine, 20 W. 43rd St., New York, NY, 10036, USA.
E. Allison Peers, *The Complete Works of St. John of the Cross*, Burns, Oates and Washbourne, 1934.
Max Picard, *The World of Silence*, H. Regnery, 1988.
Antoine de Saint-Exupéry, *The Little Prince*, Harcourt Brace and World, 1943.
William Shannon, *Thomas Merton's Dark Path*, Farrar, Straus and Giroux, 1987.
E. F. Schumacher, *Small is Beautiful*, Random House, 1989.
Madeleine Simon, *Born Contemplative*, Darton, Longman and Todd, 1993.
Cyprian Smith, *The Way of Paradox: Spiritual Life as Taught by Meister Eckhart*, Darton, Longman and Todd, 1987.
Mary Stewart and Giovanni Felicioni, *The Body in Meditation* (video), 1990.
The Tablet, 1 King St., Cloisters, Clifton Walk, London, W6 0QZ.
Mother Teresa, *Mother Teresa, Contemplative in the Heart of the World*, Servant Books, 1985.
Frank X. Tuoti, *Why Not be a Mystic?*, Crossroad, 1995.
Jean Vanier, *Talks at the 1992 John Main Seminar*, World Community for Christian Meditation.
Vatican II, Decree of the Church's Missionary Activity, *Ad Gentes*, 1965.
Vatican II, Declaration on the Relation of the Church to Non-Christian Religions, *Nostra Aetate*, 1967.
Kallistos Ware, *Theology and Prayer*, Fellowship of St Alban and St Sergius.
Ken Wilber, *Grace and Grit*, Shambhala, 1991.
Robert Wild, *Enthusiasm in the Spirit*, Ave Maria Press, 1975.
Robert Wild, *The Post Charismatic Experience*, Living Flame Press, 1984.

Name index

Abhishiktananda (Henri Le Saux) 17, 34, 84, 125
Agatho, Abba 52
Ahlften, Brigette 38
Aquinas, Thomas 34
Augustine, St 1, 3, 9, 34, 48
Baba, Meher 16
Baker, Dom Augustine 20, 34
Benedict, St 21, 29–30, 71
Benson, Dr Herbert 60
Bernard of Clairvaux, St 34, 122
Bonaventure, St 34
Buddha 93, 125
Cassian, John 6, 20, 21, 28–31, 34, 40, 47, 84, 121
Catherine of Siena 34
Chapman, Dom John 34, 40
Chrysostom, St John 34
Clark, Kenneth 21
Clement, St, of Alexandria 3, 34
Climacus, St John 34, 71
Crowley, Bishop Leonard 20
Cummings, Charles 102–4, 108

Dalai Lama 133
David, King 64
Dionysius the Areopagite 34
De Caussade, Jean Pierre 34
De Chantal, St Jane 34
de Chardin, Teilhard 34
De Foucauld, Charles 34
De Saint-Exupéry, Antoine 65
Dempsey, Jim 37

Dominion, Dr Jack 71
Dupré, Louis 72

Eastman, Patrick 26
Easwaran, Eknath 40–1, 45, 50
Eckhart, Meister 3, 17, 32, 34, 70, 89–90, 93
Elijah 23–4
Erigena, John Scotus 34
Evagrius Ponticus 3, 34
Ezekiel 65, 71, 88

Felicioni, Giovanni 56
Fitzgerald, Consilio 95–6
Francis de Sales, St 34
Francis of Assisi, St 34
Freeman, Laurence 18, 34, 49, 71, 77, 80, 85, 113, 115, 127, 130, 132

Gerard, François C. 18
Germanus 29, 121
Gilson, Etienne 34
Goldstein, Joseph 89
Gratton, Carolyn 122
Gregory of Nyssa, St 34, 74
Gregory Palamas 34
Gregory of Sinai, St 52
Gregory the Great, St 34
Griffiths, Bede 9, 34, 56, 72, 83, 84, 85–6, 133

Hamlet 134
Heron, Benedict 79
Hillesum, Etty 34
Hilton, Walter 34

NAME INDEX

Hopkins, Gerard Manley 90
Hugh of St Victor 34
Hume, Cardinal Basil 72

Irenaeus, St 4
Issac, Abba 29, 34, 121
Isaac of Syria 4
Isaiah, the Prophet 53, 105, 106, 111

James, William 34, 115
John of the Cross, St 2, 6, 16, 34, 65, 68, 102, 122
Johnston, William 33, 34, 78, 80, 87–8, 113, 133
Joseph, Abbot 74
Julian of Norwich 2, 4, 34, 72

Kazantzakis, Nikos 53
Keating, Thomas 34, 77, 79
Kiely, Robert 132
Kierkegaard, Søren 16

Lallemont, Louis 88
Law, William 34, 125
Lawrence, Brother 34
Leech, Kenneth 123
Lonergan, Bernard 34
Longfellow, Henry Wadsworth 9
Longworth, June 37
Lot, Abbot 74

Main, David and Eileen 18
Main, John ix, x, 1, 2, 3, 4, 5, 8, 9, 10, 11, 13, 15, 17, 18–22, 23, 24, 26, 28, 30, 31, 33, 34, 35, 37, 38, 40, 41, 42, 44, 46, 47, 49, 50, 52, 53, 55, 58, 59, 60, 61, 67, 68, 70, 73, 75, 77, 79, 80, 81, 82, 86, 87, 91, 92, 95, 96, 98, 99, 100, 101, 104, 112, 113, 114, 115, 117, 119, 120, 121, 122, 124, 126, 127, 129, 130, 131, 132–3, 134
Maloney, George 34

Maritain, Jacques and Raissa 34
Merton Thomas 4, 5, 34, 36, 37, 38, 62, 74, 77, 84, 89, 93, 98–9, 102, 103, 104, 106, 118, 125, 127
Miller, Annabel 72
Moses 3, 66
Murray, Pat 95–8

Nicholas of Cusa 34
Nouwen, Henri 89

Origen 34

Pascal, Blaise 34, 51, 57
Paul, St 3, 10, 11, 18, 30, 43, 46, 53, 55, 56, 59, 65, 73, 75, 92, 110, 113, 119, 120, 127
Peguy, Charles 34
Pennington, Basil 34, 77
Picard, Max 16
Po, Li 126
Polonius 134
Pythagoras 64

Rahner, Karl 34
Ramakrishna, Sri 45, 49
Rolle, Richard 57
Ruysbroeck, Jan Van 34

Sarapion the Sidonite, St 57
Satyananda, Swami 19–20
Saul, King 64
Schumacher, E. F. 115
Shannon, William 36, 93
Simon, Madeleine 63
Stein, Edith 34
Stewart, Lady Mary 56
Suso, Henry 34
Symeon, the New Theologian 34

NAME INDEX

Tauler, Johannes 32, 34
Teresa, Mother 34, 88, 90
Teresa of Avila, St 34, 49, 58, 88, 122
Thérèse of Lisieux, St 34
Theophane the Recluse 31, 34, 46
Tuoti, Frank X. 72
Tzu, Chuang 5
Tzu, Lao 52

Underhill, Evelyn 34, 73

Vanier, Jean 34, 88, 90–1, 98, 99, 100, 133
Vanier, Pauline 91
Von Hügel, Friedrich 34

Ware, Kallistos 9, 34
Weil, Simone 34, 51
Wilber, Ken 84, 126
Wild, Robert 78, 102
William of St Thierry, St 34
Wiseman, James A. 72

Yogi, Marharishi Mahesh 79

Subject index

adolescence 97
Alcoholics Anonymous 38
Aramaic (language) 11, 30, 43
attentiveness 51, 78

being (and doing) 13, 69, 76
Benedictines 20–1, 29–30, 34, 84
Bhagavad Gita 83
biblical stories 63
body 55–60
breathing 11, 55–6, 58–9
brokenness 38, 95–100
Buddhism 84–5, 89, 93, 125
busyness 25, 37, 61–2

cave of the heart 83–5, 93
charismatic movement 78–9
charisms 71
childlikeness 25
children 6, 62–3, 97
Christian Meditation: groups ix, 20, 112–16; teaching 21, 36, 115, 119–21
Christmas 15
Cistercians 36
The Cloud of Unknowing 11–12, 31–3, 38–41, 44, 52, 69
commitment 10, 23, 101–11
compassion 74, 89–91, 93
Compline (Night Prayer) 61
consciousness 17, 30; of Christ 130–1
conversion 88, 101

covetousness 48
Cuan Mhuire 95–8

death 6, 38, 127–8
desert experience 101–6
desert fathers ix, 9, 20–1, 28–31, 66, 71, 74
discipline x, 9, 46, 69, 101
distractions 11, 28–9, 41, 45, 49–55, 68
doing (and being) 13, 69, 76
double tracking 51

ego 41, 53, 68, 124–7
elitism 129
emotional wounds 95–8
Eucharist 43–4, 70–1, 75

faith 2, 14, 53–4
feelings 12, 33
feminine aspect of God 72
forgiveness 125–6, 129
formula, Cassian's 28, 30, 40, 47

Gaul 21
gender 71–2
gratitude 129–30
guilt 67, 69

harmony 31, 51, 55, 95
healing, inner 95–8
heart 9, 12–13, 26, 30, 65–6, 72

SUBJECT INDEX

Hesychast (tradition of prayer) 28–31, 66
Hinduism 83, 85
Holy Spirit 27–8, 51, 68, 71, 77, 98; fruits of the 73
humility 129–30

Ignatian exercises 77
image of God 117–19
intimacy 105

Jesuits 19
Jesus Prayer, the 30–1, 72, 86
John Main Seminar 86, 98, 100
Judaism 84, 86
justice 89

kenosis 42
Kingdom of God 1, 4, 9, 17, 24, 46
Kingdom of Heaven 23, 25
koinonia 113

L'Arche Community 89–91
Lectio Divina 120
letting go 5–7, 42, 48, 53
love 8–9, 16, 19, 31–2, 42, 61, 73, 87–91, 93, 100

mantras 1, 20–1, 28–32, 40–54, 59, 104, 119
'Maranatha' (mantra) 11, 30–1, 40, 43–4
Mary 15, 26–7
medicine 100
meditation, see Christian Meditation
metanoia 88
mind 12–13, 16, 30, 41, 49–50, 72
music 64–5
Muslims 84, 86

novenas 77

openness 8, 51, 54, 65
Orthodox Church 30, 84

other faiths 82–6

peace 28, 51
perseverance 42, 46, 52–3, 73, 101–11
philosophy 8
physiology (benefits of meditation) 60
posture 57–8
poverty of spirit 26, 47, 104
prayer ix, 1–7, 15–17, 23, 32, 61, 75–81, 120–1; prayer and action 87–94; Centering Prayer 76–7; charismatic prayer 77–9; contemplative prayer 26–7, 33, 35–9, 75–8; fruits of prayer 10, 73, 88, 91–2; liturgical prayer ix, 75, 77; petitionary prayer 75–7; trinitarian prayer 2, 4; vocal prayer 77
prayer stools 58
present, the 43
Prime (Morning Prayer) 61
Prodigal Son 118, 129
progress, spiritual 73–4
psychic phenomena 68

reality 18, 92–4
resting in God 57
rosary 77

Samaritan woman 98–100
Satan 69, 104
Scripture 23–5, 38, 73, 77, 102–4, 120–1
self-centredness 104
self-consciousness 5–7, 26, 42, 64
self, false 125–7
self-hypnosis 63–4
self-transcendence 131
self, true 125–7
senses 8
shoes 66
silence ix-x, 1–2, 4–6, 9, 15–17, 19–20, 23, 26–34, 38, 41–2,

46, 61, 69–70, 78, 83, 90–1, 113
simplicity 11–12, 26, 36, 40
sin, roots of 33
sitting 55, 57–8
Skellig Michael 21–2
sleep 67
soul friend 121–4
spiritual guides 121–4
spiritual journey 106–11
stillness ix–x, 2, 9, 16–17, 20, 26–7, 29, 32, 41, 56, 61–2, 78
surrender 26–7, 52, 69, 85

tears, gift of 71
theology 8

Transcendental Meditation (TM) 79–81
Trinity 2, 4, 19

Upanishads 20, 83, 85

Vatican Council II 83
void 69

The Way of a Pilgrim 41, 53
wholeness 31, 95–100
World Community for Christian Meditation 21, 57, 77, 98, 114, 132–3
women 71–2

yoga 56–7

The World Community for Christian Meditation

International Centre
23 Kensington Square, London W8 5HN, United Kingdom. Tel: 0171 937 4679. Fax: 0171 937 6790

Australia
Christian Meditation Community
155 Rowntree Street, Balmain 2041, Sydney, NSW. Tel: 02 810 2448.

Belgium
Christelijk Meditatie Centrum
Beiaardlaan 1, 1850 Grimbergen. Tel: 02 269 5071

Brazil
Meditacco Christa no Brasil
Nucleo Dom John Main, Caixa Postal 33266, 22442-970 Rio De Janeiro RJ, Brasil Tel: (21) 274-7104

Canada
Christian Meditation Community
P.O. Box 552, Station NDG, Montreal, Quebec H4A 3P9
Tel: 514 766 0475. Fax: 514 937 8178

John Main Centre
PO Box 56131, Ottawa, Ontario K1R 7ZO. Tel: 613 236 9437.

India
Christian Meditation Centre
1/1429 Bilathikulam Road, Calicut 673006 Kerala. Tel: 495 60395

Ireland
Christian Meditation Centre
4 Eblana Ave., Dun Laoghaire, Co. Dublin. Tel: 01 2801505

New Zealand
Christian Meditation Centre
4 Argyle Rd., Browns Bay, Auckland 1310. Tel:/Fax: 64 9 478 3438

Philippines
Christian Meditation Centre
5/f Chronicle Building, Cor. Tektite Road, Meralco Avenue/Pasig, M. Manila
Tel: 02 633 3364. Fax: 02-632 3104

WORLD COMMUNITY FOR CHRISTIAN MEDITATION

Singapore
Christian Meditation Centre
9 Mayfield St., Singapore 438 023. Tel: 65 348 6790

Thailand
Christian Meditation Centre
51/1 Sedsiri Road, Bangkok 10400. Tel: 271 3295

United Kingdom
Christian Meditation Centre
29 Campden Hill, London W8 7DX. Tel: 0171 937 0014. Fax: 0171 937 6790

United States
John Main Institute
7315 Brookville Road, Chevy Chase, MD 20815. Tel: 301 652 8635

United States
Christian Meditation Centre
1080 West Irving Park Rd., Roselle, Illinois. Tel: 708 351 2613

For a full list of all Christian Meditation Centres and Groups please write to the International Centre